The Gospel According to Tolstoy

The Gospel

According to Tolstoy

Edited and Translated by

David Patterson

The University of Alabama Press
Tuscaloosa & London

designed by zig zeigler

∞

The paper on which this book is printed
meets the minimum requirements of
American National Standard for Information
Science-Permanence of Paper for
Printed Library Materials, ANSI Z39.48-1984.

Library of Congress Cataloging-in-Publication Data

Tolstoy, Leo, graf, 1828–1910.
    [Soedinenie, perevod i issledovanie chetyrekh Evangeliĭ. En-
glish. Selections]
    The Gospel according to Tolstoy / edited and translated by David
Patterson.
        p.   cm.
    Translated selections from: Soedinenie, perevod i issledovanie
chetyrekh Evangeliĭ.
    Includes bibliographical references.
    ISBN 0-8173-0590-4
    1. Tolstoy, Leo, graf, 1828–1910—Religion.   2. Bible. N.T.
Gospels—Paraphrases, English.   I. Patterson, David, 1948–   .
II. Title.
BS2555.T6452213   1992
226'.06—dc20   92-16290

British Library Cataloguing-in-Publication Data available

For Dan and Don

Contents

Translator's Introduction

Y THE FALL of 1879, the fifty-one-year old author of *War and Peace* (1869) and *Anna Karenina* (1877) had arrived at the dreadful conviction that he had accomplished nothing of value in life, that his life was evil and meaningless. Seeking a way to emerge from his tomb of despair, he set his pen to a work later titled *Confession*, which laid the foundations for the spiritual path he would pursue until the end of his life in 1910. In that work, Tolstoy wrote, "It is clear that I do not live whenever I lose my faith in the existence of God, and I would have killed myself long ago if I did not have some vague hope of finding God. I truly live only when I am conscious of Him and seek Him. 'What, then, do I seek?' a voice cried out within me, 'He is there, the one without whom there could be no life.' To know God and to live come to one and the same thing. God is life. 'Live, seeking God, for there can be no life without God.' And more powerfully than ever a light shone within me and all around me, and this light has not abandoned me since" (74–75). A personal, impassioned tale of the great author's plunge into despair and his struggle to rise again, the *Con-*

fession was intended to be an introduction to three subsequent works: A *Critique of Dogmatic Theology* (1880–83),
What I Believe (1883–84), and A *Harmony, Translation, and
Investigation of the Four Gospels* (1880–91). This third piece is
among Tolstoy's most ambitious searches for God, for himself, and for the nature of truth. In 1891, his friend Pavel
Ivanovich Biryukov took the work to Geneva, where it was
first published in Russian in three volumes; it came out again
(also in Russian) in the "Svobodnago Slova" ["Free Word"]
Edition published at Christchurch, England, in 1906. This
work is a further elaboration of the piece that appears in
volume 24 of the Jubilee Edition under the title A *Harmony
and Translation of the Four Gospels*. Since the "Free Word"
Edition is closer to what ultimately came from Tolstoy's hand,
I have selected it as the basis for what is here presented as
The Gospel According to Tolstoy.

In his article "Tolstoy and the Greek Gospel," David
Redston notes that Tolstoy taught himself Greek in the winter
of 1870–71 (21), a point that indicates Tolstoy's desire to
master that language of the Gospels long before he undertook
an analytical study of them. His first mention of A *Harmony,
Translation, and Investigation of the Four Gospels* appears in a
letter he wrote to Nikolai Nikolaich Strakhov on 26(?) Sep-
tember 1880 (*Letters*, 338); later that year, on 28(?) December, he again reported to Strakhov on the project, noting,
"I would say I am half way through. And everything becomes
brighter and brighter as the work goes on" (*Letters*, 339);
indeed, the work did go on for more than ten years. In A
Harmony, Translation, and Investigation of the Four Gospels,
Tolstoy examines selected passages from the Greek Scriptures, accompanied by the Russian Orthodox translation,
and then he offers his own Russian translation of the texts,
with an explanation and justification of how he arrived at his
version. His analysis of the Orthodox rendition of the Scrip-

tures includes a scathing critique of the Orthodox interpretation of the Gospels written by a man whom he identifies as
Archimandrite Mikhail; this is very likely the same Mikhail
(Desnitsky) who worked on the Russian translation of the
Gospels produced by the Russian Bible Society in 1821 under
the auspices of Alexander I (see Tal'berg, 816–17). Tolstoy's
investigation also addresses commentaries of the Gospels
written by his European contemporaries, most notably
French Catholic Edouard Reuss (1804–91). Combining his
critique of prevailing interpretations with an etymological
study of the Greek texts, he concludes each chapter with an
edited narrative based on the passages in question. These
summaries comprising the life and teachings of Jesus have
been gathered into this volume to form *The Gospel According
to Tolstoy.*

We have in hand, then, an edited and translated version of
the Gospels edited and translated by Tolstoy, not only as he
understood them but as he wished to have them understood.
Before addressing the problematic nature of reading such a
text, however, we must first establish the philosophical and
theological contexts for it.

Philosophical and Theological Contexts

Looking more closely at the passage from the *Confession*
cited above, one will note that, for Tolstoy, knowing God and
choosing life come to the same thing; to name and thus comprehend the Nameless One became for him a matter not only
of life and death but of salvation and damnation. But because
God *is* the Nameless One, Tolstoy realized that the essence of
life lay not so much in the name as in the struggle to name
and thus to understand. "I can neither understand nor name
Him," he writes in *The Concept of God* (1897). "If I were to

understand Him, then I would attain Him; there would be
nothing left to strive for, and there would be no life. . . . Any
intelligible representation of what I know to be God (for
example, that He is the Creator, is merciful, and so on) dis-
tances me from Him" (3–4). This accent on seeking rather
than finding is part of the philosophical outlook that Tolstoy
brings to his reading of the Gospels. As Richard F. Gustafson
has pointed out in his study of the Russian author's fiction
and theology, "Tolstoy found justification for his theological
views in the Gospels, but his interpretation of the Gospels
rests on attitudes and assumptions which he discovered
within himself and then brought to the texts" (191). Tolstoy's
version of the Gospels is much more than a translation of the
Greek texts; it is a philosophical interpretation of those texts
that transforms the Greek word into a Tolstoyan idea. Going
beyond the traditional account of the life and teachings of
Jesus, Tolstoy here produces a treatise on his own understanding of the truth and meaning of life. "There is only one
eternal, universal, world-wide teaching of the truth," he
wrote in his diary on 2 December 1897, "as expressed particularly clearly for me and for us all in the Gospels" (*Diaries*,
451). This "for me," however, is positioned over against the
authoritative word of the other as represented by the Church
and the institutions it sanctions. In *Resurrection* (1899), for
example, Tolstoy invokes the Gospel as the basis for his attack
on the Church; it stands above his polemic as the position
from which the truth of his own position is determined. One
place in the novel where he sets up the opposition between
the truth of the Gospel and the lie of Orthodoxy is in the
very midst of a prison church service, which he describes by
saying,

To none of the participants, from the priest and the superinten-
dent to Maslova, did it occur that Jesus himself—whose name

the priest endlessly repeated in wheezing tones, praising him
with all sorts of strange words—had forbidden precisely what
was being done here; that he had forbidden not only the meaningless babble and the blasphemous incantation of priests and
teachers over bread and wine, but in the most explicit terms had
forbidden one group of people to refer to others as their teachers;
that he had forbidden prayers in temples and had commanded
each person to pray in solitude; that he had forbidden temples
themselves, saying that he had come to destroy them and that one
must pray not in temples but in spirit and in truth; and that,
above all, he had not only forbidden judging people and holding
them in confinement, torturing, humiliating, and executing them
as it was done here, but he had come to set free those who were
captive. (143–44)

As in his rendition of the Gospels, Tolstoy here engages the
Church with a different reading of the very text that it pre-
tends to follow. What he attributes to the Gospels, again,
comes from himself. The prayer he would have uttered
according to the spirit arises from a reading according to the
letter.

The key to Tolstoy's interpretation of the truth of the Gospels lies in his translation of a single word, the Greek word
logos. Normally rendered as "the Word," or *slovo* in Russian,
logos in Tolstoy's Gospel is translated as *razumenie*, a term that
is usually taken to mean "understanding," "intelligence," or
"comprehension." Examining the roots of the word *razumenie*,
we find in it suggestions of *um*, *razum*, and *umenie*, which
mean "mind," "reason," and "intellectual ability," respec-
tively. Tolstoy believed that anyone who is endowed with even
a rudimentary capacity for thought is capable of receiving the
truth of the Gospels. "There is no teaching more immoral
and harmful," he contends in *On Reason, Faith, and Prayer*
(1900), "than the teaching that man cannot achieve perfection by his own strength"; this is precisely the teaching that

"reason is not sufficient for understanding the truth, that external, indubitable proofs are needed" (9–10). The form of reason he has in mind is not that process or method through which one might generate proofs; rather, it is a capacity for an immediate seeing or direct perception of the truth as it is spelled out in the text. This is the form of reason that is the touchstone for his investigation of the four Gospels. He explains that he settles on *razumenie* as a translation of *logos* because it is not only reason but the action whereby reason provides a direction for the human being, enabling a person to act in truth and in goodness. The action of reason's conviction, in Tolstoy's view, amounts to the faith that he describes in the *Confession* as "the force of life": "Faith lies not only in the 'manifestation of things unseen' and so on, or in revelation (this is simply a description of one of the signs of faith); nor is it simply the relation between man and God (faith must first be determined and then God, not the other way around), or agreeing with what one has been told, even though this is often what it is understood to be. Faith is the knowledge of the meaning of human life, whereby the individual does not destroy himself but lives. Faith is the force of life" (61). Life is, above all, movement, he argues in *The Kingdom of God Is within You* (1893), from darkness to light, from lower truth to higher truth (402). And the impetus underlying that movement is the *logos* or capacity for *razumenie* that is at the heart of any being who is human.

Faith and reason, therefore, are not opposed to each other in Tolstoy's scheme of religious life. Both constitute the living presence that animates man as it unveils God. God is revealed through his disturbance of the witness; first came the wings and then the angel, first the light and then the fire. To be sure, God created light before he created the fires of the firmament; the light is what makes the fire visible, even as it emanates from the flame. In a similar way, Tolstoy asserts, "like man and his power of reason, the knowledge of faith arises from a mysterious origin. This origin is God, the source of the human mind and body" (*Confession*, 78). God imparts life by imparting that faith and reason through which he manifests himself; God imparts life by imparting meaning to life and with it an understanding of life. The person in whom faith lives is not so much one who feels or even one who believes as one who understands. And where understanding *(razumenie)* is at work, reason *(razum)* is at work. For Tolstoy, then, to say that Jesus is the way, the truth, and the light is to say that Jesus is the understanding, the one who opens up the path that faith is to follow. "Only life founded on the Understanding," says Tolstoy, "reveals the way to God" (*Harmony*, 47), because only understanding can direct the faith that is the force of life toward truth. "Whether we like it or not," Tolstoy insists, "no truth can enter the soul of man without reason" (*Reason*, 13). If reason determines the structure of our relations with God and with one another, truth is the measure of the substance of those relations. And truth is another term for the will of God. Since truth enters the human soul through reason, "reason," Tolstoy maintains, "reveals to man the will of God, of the one who sent him into the world" (*Reason*, 3). One will note here a significant change in Tolstoy's view of reason as it is represented in *Anna Karenina*, for example, where we read, "Reason discovered the struggle for existence and the law demanding the suffocation of all who hinder the satisfaction of my desires. This is the conclusion of reason" (422). The change from this position to what we find in his later works was the result of his examination of Christ as *logos* and of truth as the will of God.

Although "reason is given to all of us from God," as Tolstoy says (*Reason*, 5), it is received only through our response to God, in our declaration of "Here I am," by which we come to life in our consciousness of life. "The life in me is conscious-

ness," Tolstoy declares in *The Concept of God*. "This consciousness is God. . . . That which imparts consciousness to
me is Reason. Reason is my enlightenment through consciousness" (12–13). In his *Thoughts on God* (1901), he expresses it by saying, "No matter how much what we call the
'world'—our relation to the world—may change, one thing is
undoubtedly beyond change in our knowing the world: it is
that which knows. . . . This thing which knows is everywhere
one; it is in all things and in itself. This is God. And that part
of God which is somehow contained constitutes our genuine
I" (33). The idea that God is somehow contained—that
within is in some way tied to *above*—implies that the finite
may somehow become a vessel of the infinite, a part of the all
couched in the particular. In the human realm, this notion
underlies Tolstoy's view of every human being as a son of God.
Thus, as Gustafson has shown, "The evangelical 'names'—
God, Spirit, Son of God, Son of Man, light, and understanding—Tolstoy insists, all refer to the same 'basic concept,' but
seen from various points of view. 'When it is spoken of as the
principle *(nachalo)* of everything, it is called *God;* when it is
spoken of in relation to the flesh, it is *Spirit;* when it is spoken
of in relation to its source, it is named the *Son of God;* when it
is spoken of as its manifestation, it is named *Son of Man;*
when it is spoken of as compliance to its reason, it is named
light and understanding'" (91). The key phrase in Tolstoy's
assessment of the various names of God is "in relation to."
Placing his accent on relation, Tolstoy takes up a view of the
Gospels that endeavors to unveil the basis of all these relations.

"Why does God divide Himself within Himself?" Tolstoy
asks in *Thoughts on God*. "I do not know. But I know that it is
so, that in this is life. All that we know is nothing other than
a division of God. All that we know as the world is a knowledge of these divisions" (34). Chief among those divisions or

particularities through which we know God, of course, is he who reveals the will of God, the Christ-logos who abides in all things, in all people—a position that leads Tolstoy to reject the equation of Jesus with God. In a letter to Hamilton Campbell, a minister of the Free Church of Scotland, dated 27 January–6 February 1891, he asserts, "Christ being God is a belief that can be kept only by people who do not want to accept his teaching, . . . which cannot be accepted by clergy because it destroys at once their position and shows that their vocation is only a pretense to feed at the cost of the people" (*Letters,* 475). The significance of Jesus, as Tolstoy sees it, is that he manifests the divine presence within each of us by which we may overcome death. The portion of the Gospels that Tolstoy omits lies outside of the teachings of the texts and belongs to the externals of miracle, mystery, and authority, by which dogma would enslave and finally destroy the soul. Getting rid of the God in the God-man, Tolstoy opens up the God in every man, for whatever comes at the expense of a single human being comes in a rejection of God. Such a reconstruction of the teaching leads to a deconstruction of the Teacher as dogma would represent—or misrepresent—him. Tolstoy states it quite simply in *On Reason, Faith, and Prayer:* "To acknowledge Christ as God is to reject God" (13). For to invest one human being with divinity to the exclusion of others is to deny the inner, divine aspect that makes each individual a human being. Although this may not be the view of most believers with regard to the Christ, Tolstoy appears to read the doctrine in this manner. The acknowledgment of Jesus as God, then, is not only a rejection of God but of man as well, of the one formed in the image of God. In short, it robs the finite of the element of the infinite that alone gives it meaning. "In order for a man to live," we recall the line from the *Confession,* "he must have an explanation of the meaning of life by which the finite and the infinite would be equated"

(61). While Tolstoy refuses the identification of Jesus with God, therefore, he does not reject the divinity of Jesus any more than he would reject the divine element in any human being. Hence, Tolstoy displaces the Christ of dogmatic theology with a Christ perfectly in keeping with his own theology, in keeping, perhaps, with the image of what he himself would become.

Tolstoy understands the union of Father and Son posited in the Gospels as a union of the inner, divine essence of humanity with the essence of the divinity, so that the phrase "Son of God" is an expression of every human being's relation to the Holy One (see *Kingdom*, 113). "This living entity," he writes in *The Concept of God*, "which man senses in himself imparts to him life and joy in life; this is the 'Son of God' in man" (10)—not God, be it noted, but the *Son* of God, a distinction that would dispel any heretical equation of man with God. The Son is not the same as the Father but has within him a part of the Father that is as definitive to his identity as a genetic imprint. Indeed, this parallel with an imprint is extremely suggestive; just as he who reads the Gospels in truth reads the truth of himself, so does the imprint on the scriptural page uncover the imprint on the self, the sign that distinguishes the soul as divine. "I cannot understand myself," says Tolstoy in *Thoughts on God*, "except as a part of Him" (14). From the standpoint of Tolstoy's theology, the concept of God is tied to a concept of the self, with each deriving its sense from its relation to the other. And the middle term in that relation is the Christ-logos of the Gospel according to Tolstoy. Although such a notion of Jesus runs contrary to traditional Christian views, it is more distant from the Western than from the Eastern concept of the Christ. According to Western theology, Christ as God-man takes on all human sin and offers himself as a sacrifice to bring about the atonement of God and humanity. The Eastern conception is that Christ vanquishes death and the forces of evil that hold people captive, a view that is much closer to Tolstoy's thinking. And the thing that sets people free is truth, the truth of understanding. Says Tolstoy in *The Kingdom of God Is within You,* "For every man there are always truths that are invisible to him, that are not yet revealed to his intellectual faculty. There are other truths already experienced, forgotten, or mastered by him; and there are known truths that have risen up by the light of his reason and demand to be acknowledged. In the recognition or nonrecognition of these truths there appears what we know as our freedom" (401–2). Thus, Tolstoy posits not only a freedom to act but a freedom to respond in the light of a given responsibility; that responsibility is the basis of the freedom introduced by Jesus.

The divisions of God within himself cited above thus lead us to a life that inheres in a difference that is a nonindifference: being-in-God means being-for-the-other, responsible to God for the welfare of the other. This is precisely the difficulty addressed in Tolstoy's short novel *Father Sergius* (1898). Pleased with his influence on people, the title character "thought about the fact that he was a glowing lamp, and the more he felt this, the more he felt a weakening, an extinguishing of the divine light of truth that burned within him. 'How much of what I do is for God, and how much is for people?'—that was the question that constantly tormented him and which he was not so much unable to answer as he was unable to confront the answer within himself" (329). In the end, however, Father Sergius realizes that his difficulty arises from a position of I-for-myself, which excludes both God and human beings, making them into objects for one's own glorification. From his friend Pashenka he learns that he must transform this I-for-myself into an I-for-the-other that includes both God and human beings. "I had lived for people," he says, "under the pretense of living for God, while she lives for God, imagining that she lives for people. . . . There is no God for one who lives, as I did, for human glory" (345). There, where being-for-the-other is being-for-God, the finite becomes a vessel of the infinite. When the relation to the human Thou is a manifestation of the relation to the Eternal Thou, the divine aspect of the I comes into communication with the divine aspect of the Thou. For Tolstoy, as Gustafson notes, "the concept of God as an abstract idea of absolute being has been replaced by a God who dwells in the world of change even as He transcends it" (108)—where the world of change is the world of human life and interaction, of transitions from birth to death to rebirth.

The idea of being-for-the-other is particularly prominent in Tolstoy's *Resurrection,* where the novel's main character, Nekhlyudov, realizes that freedom lies not in doing whatever you want to do but in realizing what you *must* do. Freedom, in other words, does not mean being the master of oneself but the servant of God, as Nekhlyudov discovers: "'Yes,' it occurred to him, 'to feel oneself not the master but a servant,' and that thought filled him with joy" (235). Thus, the character sets out to live the idea expressed by his author in *Thoughts on God,* where we read, "People know two Gods: one whom they want to force to serve them through prayers demanding from Him the fulfillment of their desires—and another God, whom we must serve, the fulfillment of whose will must determine the direction of our lives" (35). How does Nekhlyudov assume the status of God's servant? By serving others: this lived theology, which characterizes Tolstoy's religious thought, is brought to life in the offering up of one's life for the sake of the other in the realization that the path to God leads through the human being before us. "God does His work through us," says Tolstoy (*Thoughts,* 36), and God is able to work through us only when we become as nothing before him and thus as an opening through which he may pass into the world. Mikhail Bakhtin expresses it by saying, "What I must be for the other is what God is for me" (*Estetika*, 52). In *Resurrection*, then, everything becomes clear to Nekhlyudov "because he was not thinking of what would become of himself—he had no interest in this—but he was thinking only of what he must do. And, surprising as it may seem, although there was no way he could determine what was needful for himself, he knew without a doubt what was needful for others" (234). Thus, setting out to act on behalf of the other, Nekhlyudov ultimately returns to himself with a self. Signifying the dearness and the depth of the other, he takes on a depth, a significance, of his own; standing before the other, he stands for a responsibility that is beyond both himself and the other.

This notion of responsibility returns us once again to a concept of life as it is lived *in relation*, and it introduces to relation a dialogical aspect with respect to the words and deeds that constitute human interaction. "According to the teaching of the Scribes," Tolstoy notes in *A Harmony, Translation, and Investigation of the Four Gospels*, "people are the slaves of God, and are not free; but according to the teaching of Jesus Christ, people are free" (106). The teaching of the scribes is a teaching that prescribes, opposing monological dictum to dialogical interaction. With the coming of Jesus, the dictatorial God is eclipsed by the God who resides in relation: "Henceforth God is no longer the inaccessible God that He was before, but God will be in the world and in the interactions among people. If God is in the world and in the interactions among people, then what sort of God is He? Is He God the Creator, who sits in heaven, who revealed Himself to the Patriarchs and gave His Law to Moses, the tormenting, cruel, and terrible God whom people knew and revered; or is this another God? . . . Jesus determines that this is not God" (*Harmony,* 113). It should be pointed out before going any further that Tolstoy does not so much replace a monological authority with a dialogical approach to truth as set up a new, self-styled authoritative voice supported by his own reading of the Gospels. And one could put together a sound argument that in his reading of the Gospels he has misread the Scriptures of the Old Testament, the God of which is not merely "cruel, tormenting, and terrible." Nevertheless, it is worth noting that his dismissal of the Hebrew God is reminiscent of that heretical form of Christianity outlined by Marcion in the second century. Establishing a church of his own, Marcion taught that Christianity has no connection with Judaism, and he rejected the canon of Hebrew Scriptures. Much like Tolstoy, in fact, Marcion compiled his own Gospel, omitting the infancy narrative, Christ's genealogy, his baptism, and his temptation in the wilderness. Unlike Marcion, however, in his own time, Tolstoy appears to be the only major figure, at least in Russian circles, to adopt this stance toward the God of Abraham.

Tolstoy's apparent embrace of dialogical freedom over monological power comes more as a justification for his own attack on dogmatic theology than as a new dialogical outlook on the truth. Underlying his attack is a position very similar to the one expressed by Carl Jung when he writes, "What is usually called 'religion' is to such an amazing degree a substitute that I ask myself seriously whether this kind of 'religion,' which I prefer to call a creed, has not an important function in human society. The substitution has the obvious purpose of replacing immediate experience by a choice of suitable symbols invested in a solidly organized dogma or ritual. The Catholic church maintains them by her indisputable authority, the Protestant church (if this term is still applicable) by insistence on faith and the evangelical message. As long as these two principles work, people are effectively de-

fended and shielded against immediate religious experience"
(52–53). The deception Jung describes is not as innocuous as
he might make it seem, since it entails a betrayal of all that
sanctifies life. Recall, for example, Tolstoy's assertion in his
Critique of Dogmatic Theology: "I remember that before I
doubted the teaching of the Church and was reading the
Gospel, I could not at all understand these words: 'Whoever
says a word against the Son of Man will be forgiven; but
whoever speaks against the Holy Spirit will not be forgiven,
either in this age or in the age to come.' Now these words are
all too terribly clear to me. This is the word uttered against
the Holy Spirit, which will not be forgiven either in this age
or in the age to come: it is the teaching of the Church"
(314–15). Earlier on, in the *Confession*, Tolstoy wrote that
when he considered "what is done in the name of religion,"
he "was horrified and very nearly withdrew from the Orthodox Church entirely" (88). At that time, the thing about the
Church that most disturbed him was its approval of wars and
executions (*Confession*, 89), but this concern soon led him to
other, deeper concerns. Among the false and insidious teachings of the Church, he realized, was the proposition that only
through the Church could people understand and draw near
to God, that one group of people can and must dominate
another in order to serve God.

And so in the *Critique of Dogmatic Theology*, he insists that
"everything in the word *Church* amounts to another name for
a deception by which some people want to have power over
others" (323). Having turned away from the teaching of Jesus
that Tolstoy would restore, "the Church," he argues, "has
twisted it into a negation of all life: instead of poverty it
fosters luxury; instead of non-judgment, the most cruel judgment; instead of forgiveness for offenses, hatred and wars;
instead of the non-resistance of evil, executions" (322). In
Resurrection, this criticism becomes a motif. In a description

of the attending priest at Maslova's trial, for instance, we read, "He was very proud of having sworn in several tens of thousands of men and of continuing to serve in his declining years the glory of his Church, fatherland, and family, to which, in addition to a house, he would leave capital amounting to thirty thousand rubles in securities. It never occurred to him that his work in the court, which consisted of having people swear oaths on the Gospel that forbids them, was not good" (33). Just as Judas betrays Jesus for thirty pieces of silver, so this priest betrays him for thirty thousand. As for the head of the Church itself, Tolstoy provides us with a portrait of Pobedonostsev through the character Toporov, who, like Pobedonostsev, is the head of the Holy Synod. "The post held by Toporov," he relates, "involved an inner contradiction which only a stupid person void of moral sensibility could fail to see. Toporov possessed both of these negative characteristics" (305). The contradiction is that the Church, which, according to its own doctrine, was established and upheld by God, requires human intervention, including violence, in order to survive. Furthermore, like other priests in the novel, Toporov "was not a believer and found such a condition very comfortable and pleasant" (306). By now it is easy to see why it became a crime to read or possess most of Tolstoy's religious works in tsarist Russia, but the tsar left Tolstoy himself alone, refusing to add the jewel of martyrdom to his crown of glory. "The only respectable residence for an honest man in Russia today is prison," Nekhlyudov reflects in the novel *Resurrection* (314), but Tolstoy was not to enjoy that honor.

Tolstoy believed that the Gospel itself, in fact, rejects all earthly authority, both religious and political. Among the five rules for living set down by Tolstoy's Jesus is the injunction to make no distinctions between one nation and another, that is, to acknowledge no kings or kingdoms. The other four rules are moral prohibitions against anger, adultery, oaths, and the judgment of others; at the end of *Resurrection,* it will be recalled, Nekhlyudov arrives at a variation of these five rules as he discovers them in the fifth chapter of the Gospel according to Saint Matthew (see 456–57). Coupling a theological outlook with a moral stance, Tolstoy promotes a way of knowledge that is typical of Russian thought. "With his fellow Russians," Gustafson observes, "Tolstoy firmly believes that right knowledge requires moral goodness" (461). Among those fellow Russians who maintain such views are Vladimir Solovev (1853–1900), Nikolai Berdyaev (1874–1948), Simon Frank (1877–1950), and Pavel Florensky (1882–1943). In an attempt to join right knowledge with moral action, Tolstoy made certain changes in his own life during the 1880s: he refused jury service, became a vegetarian, renounced all blood sports, and gave up alcohol and tobacco. Yet it would be a mistake to declare that Tolstoy wanted to translate faith only into such externals. As he puts it in *The Kingdom of God Is within You,* "the teaching of Christ is distinguished from previous teachings by the fact that it guides people not by external rules but by an internal consciousness of the possibility of attaining divine perfection" (112). Tolstoy's interest, then, lies not only in the truth of deeds but also in the spirit of truth; he is as much concerned with the inner life as with the outer action. The essence of the inward, spiritual life, he believes, is love. Embracing Jesus' statement in John 13:35, Tolstoy insists that the one mark of the Christian is his or her capacity for love. Love is the substance of the spirit and of God; it is the way, the truth, and the life. He who knows, knows truth; he who knows truth, knows love.

To live according to the will of God, as Tolstoy understands it, is to live according to truth, reason, and, above all, love. In the language of Tolstoy's religious discourse, love is the definitive element, the very essence, of consciousness. Hence, he writes, "the emergence of consciousness in me lies in loving, in serving, people; not in regarding those dictates of consciousness which poison pleasures as unhappiness but, on the contrary, in regarding them as salvation—in a word, this emergence of consciousness is *reason*" (*Concept,* 14). The salvation born of understanding is the salvation that arises from the loving consciousness of the other, both as person and as God. If it is the case, as Tolstoy claims, that "when I am conscious, I am no longer *I* but am a single consciousness" (*Concept,* 15), this unity is the unity of I-and-Thou joined in love. Since the consciousness of the other human being is a consciousness of God, so is the love for the other a love for God. In this unity, we have the oneness of the God who is love: he who loves, loves God. "If," Tolstoy declares, "someone says, 'I love God but I hate my brother,' he is a liar"; hence, "he who dwells in love abides in God, and God is in him" (*Reason,* 17). Love is not one feeling among many but a living presence between two. In the words of Martin Buber, "feelings one 'has'; love occurs. Feelings dwell in man, but man dwells in his love. This is no metaphor but actuality; love does not cling to an I, as if the You were merely its 'content' or object; it is between I and You" (66). Life, therefore, is not just in me or in the other but is in *between,* where God is present, is *presence,* as the essence and origin of life. "And we know that we pass from death to life," Tolstoy asserts, "if we love our brother. He who does not love his brother has no eternal life in him" (*Reason,* 19). In this definitive union of love with life, *between* and *within* become synonyms. The love that is God, which makes the *between* into a manifestation of the *within,* is a "love for love," as Tolstoy describes it in *The Concept of God,* "that very goodness, kindness, and joy which is man's own true, blessed life, which knows not death" (4–5). If God is love—if "that is, we know God," says Tolstoy, "only in the form of love" (*Thoughts,* 38)—then that love by which

God is known is a knowing of God by himself. We think we love God by loving our neighbor, and this is surely the case, but it is not entirely the case. For the love with which we love God is itself divine. "God can never be object," to draw on an insight from Paul Tillich, "without being at the same time subject" (11). Again, in this oneness lies the oneness of God, his simultaneous presence within and transcendence of the world.

In the Hebrew Scriptures, the ineffable name of God, the *yud-hey-vav-hey* of the tetragrammaton, contains all the tenses of the Hebrew verb *to be;* in the Holy Name, *was, is,* and *will be* are gathered into one. The name from which Tolstoy seeks a life that is not destroyed by death is this name that signifies both presence and transcendence. When Tolstoy states that God is "the beginning of beginnings" (*Thoughts,* 10), he has in mind not only the beginning that was but the beginning that is and ever shall be the beginning. The life that has its origin from God is a life in which nothing ends and everything begins. If to live is to seek God, as Tolstoy asserted in the *Confession* (74–75), then to seek God is to love, to begin ever again from the wellspring of love, and thus to continually unearth one's own soul. While dogmatic theology condemns all those who do not conform to the dogma, Tolstoy believes that in love he has found the essence of all religions. And so, when Nekhlyudov asks the old tramp in *Resurrection* why there are different religions, he gets this Tolstoyan reply:

> There are different religions because people believe in other people but don't believe in themselves. I used to believe in people, and I went astray, like I was lost in a great forest. I got so lost that I thought I would never find my way out. There were Old Believers and New Believers and Sabbaterians and Khlysti and Papists and Anti-Papists and Austrians and Molokans and Skoptsy. Each belief has praise only for itself. And so they all

crawl around like blind puppies. There are many beliefs, but the
spirit is one. In you, in me, and in him. It means that if each
believes his own spirit, then all will be united. If each is himself,
then all will be one. . . . I have no name, no place, no land—no
nothing. . . . I always was and I always will be. . . . I have no
father or mother, except for God and the earth. (431)

Such is the negation of self by which a human being becomes
a self through his relation to another. The oneness of body
and spirit, the openness of God, unfolds in this union of self
and other, self and God, self and itself. Just as there is one
truth and one spirit, there is but one love. The two commandments that sum up the whole of the law—to love God and to
love one's fellow human being—are, according to Tolstoy, of a
piece. And he who loves God by loving his fellow human being
is a follower of Christ, a temple where the spirit of truth
dwells.

Here we have the key to Tolstoy's notion of "human
participation in the divine," as Gustafson puts it, "which is
modeled on the Platonic *methexis* of particular things in the
idea," and "reflects Tolstoy's Eastern Christian understanding of man's relationship to God. In brief, this tradition portrays a human being who shares in the divine qualities, but
who attains his true humanity and thus participates in the
Divine only when he himself manifests those qualities"
(93–94). Just as Tolstoy attempts to eliminate vague abstrac-
tions that stand in the way of a rational acceptance of the
Gospel, so does he exclude those points of doctrine that
obstruct a loving relation to one's neighbor. Christianity,
Tolstoy believes, has nothing to do with the dogma that walks
in long robes; Christianity is about living a life rooted in love,
not in an institution or theological tract. It is about the truth
that Ivan Il'ich discovers as he is dying at the end of Tolstoy's
Death of Ivan Il'ich (1886):

"Yes, none of it has been what was needful," he said to himself, "but that doesn't matter. It can, the 'needful' thing can be done. But what is the 'needful' thing?" he asked himself and suddenly fell silent. This was at the end of the third day, an hour before his death. At that moment the schoolboy quietly crept toward his father and went up to his bed. The dying man was still crying out in despair and waving his hands. His hand fell on the schoolboy's head. The schoolboy caught it, pressed it to his lips, and started weeping. At that moment Ivan Il'ich fell through and saw the light, and it was revealed to him that his life had not been what was needful and that it was still possible to correct. He asked himself: "What, indeed, is 'needful'?" And he fell silent, listening intensely. Then he felt someone kissing his hand. He opened his eyes and caught sight of his son. (228–29)

How is the light of life revealed through the darkness of death? Not through text or treatise but in the touch of a child and the compassion of the face in its exposure to the hand it would kiss. Like an echo of silence in the midst of words, the kiss silently reveals more than the word can convey and all that Tolstoy would convey in his rendition of the Gospel, which is centered on the human not as something opposed to the divine but as the portal to the divine. If Tolstoy's *Confession* marks a turning point in the direction of his writing, his version of the Gospel provides the key to reading between the lines of those texts that followed the *Confession*. And so we come to the question of how to read the Gospel according to Tolstoy.

Tolstoy's Method of Reading and a Method of Reading Tolstoy

Gustafson has shown that Tolstoy not only excluded "the Old Testament from scriptural revelation," but he also purged

"the Gospels of what he did not need or find intelligible. . . .
The essence of Christianity, purged of mystery and the
Hebraic tradition, lay for Tolstoy in an ethic and metaphysics
of love. This love is God and the logos of the world" (190). It
will be noted immediately that Tolstoy's Christ is not the
Messiah foretold by the prophets, and like Marcion, he omits
anything from his Gospel that might link Jesus with the
messianic house of David and thereby create the illusion of
justification for a pseudobelief in him. We have discussed
Tolstoy's religious concept of love; what we must do here is
determine how his notion of the intelligible affects his method
of interpreting the Gospels. Taking this notion as his point of
reference, Tolstoy edits and translates the Gospels so that they
might be in harmony not only with each other but with his own
philosophical position. Rather than simply read the Gospels in
an attempt to understand them as a unified text, he reads *into*
them by extracting *from* them all that, in his words, is "sufficient and understandable for the meek and the slow-witted,
over against the wise men and scholars" (*Critique,* 321). Un-
dertaking his effort to translate—to *perevodit'* or "lead across,"
as the Russian verb suggests—Tolstoy "leads" his reader
"across" the Greek and Russian Orthodox versions of the text
to arrive at what he takes to be clear and distinct by the natural
light of his own reasoning, his own *razumenie.* This method, he
believes, will free a reading of the Gospels from the ideology of
power that the Church reads into it and will penetrate the true
meaning of the Greek text. Positioning the Russian Orthodox
text alongside the Greek original, then, he opposes truth to
authority by introducing the authority of his own reason. This
too marks a departure from a method suggested in the *Confession,* where Tolstoy writes, "I know that the explanation of
all things, like the origin of all things, must remain hidden in
infinity. But I do want to understand in order that I might be
brought to the inevitably incomprehensible; I want all that is

incomprehensible to be such not because the demands of the intellect are not sound (they are sound, and apart from them I understand nothing) but because I perceive the limits of the intellect. I want to understand, so that any instance of the incomprehensible occurs as a necessity of reason and not as an obligation to believe" (90–91). By the time Tolstoy takes up his reading and rendition of the Gospel, he allows little room for the inevitably incomprehensible. The revelation he seeks belongs not to the mysterious but to common sense as he understands it.

Thus, in his investigation of the Gospels, Tolstoy adopts the method that he prescribes to a student from Kharkov named Nikolai Vasilevich Mikhailov in a letter dated 16 February 1889: "As you read them, first strike out the passages in which Christ is spoken about, leaving the ones in which Christ speaks himself. Then divide up Christ's words themselves, marking off all that is incomprehensible, unclear, contradictory, or even seemingly so, leaving the passages which are absolutely clear. You must read these passages over and over again, trying to unite them into one whole, and then, having mastered this whole, having mastered the spirit of the teaching, read through the unclear passages again, trying to understand them too, but in no way forcing the sense; better to leave in something incomprehensible than to make strained interpretations" (*Letters*, 440). Strained interpretations here include anything that belongs to indirect or multivoiced discourse. His aim is to close what Bakhtin calls "the loophole left open" when the latter says, "This potential other meaning, that is, the loophole left open, accompanies the word like a shadow. Judged by its meaning alone, the word with a loophole should be an ultimate word and does present itself as such, but in fact it is only the penultimate word and places after itself only a conditional, not a final, period" (*Problems*, 233). Rejecting such a word, Tolstoy is after the "hagiographic word," which he reads according to his own word. "The hagiographic word," Bakhtin explains, "is a word without a sideward glance, calmly adequate to itself and to its referential object" (*Problems*, 248). The greatest threat to the hagiographic word, as Tolstoy sees it, is the discourse of the incomprehensible that Church dogma would impose on the text in order to win the faith of the convert and thus wield its own authority. For Tolstoy, what is chiefly incomprehensible, contradictory, and inimical to the teaching of Jesus is anything that pertains to the miraculous; indeed, much of his conclusion to this investigation of the Gospels is devoted to an argument against the Resurrection, which he regards as the most offensive of the miracles. The Gospel according to Tolstoy, therefore, contains no miracles, nothing that does not lend itself to rational understanding; even the parables he retains are drained of anything that might hint at the esoteric. "I think that to accept or to believe in the miracles of the Gospel is a complete impossibility for a sane person in our times," he wrote in his letter to Hamilton Campbell. "I think that the faith in the miracle excludes the faith in the teaching" (*Letters*, 474–75). For faith in the teaching is, again, faith in *razumenie*.

Five years after completing his translation of the Gospels, Tolstoy wrote a short piece titled *How to Read the Gospel* (1896), in which he prescribes a revisionary, red-letter method of reading before any red-letter editions of the Gospels had appeared: "Let anyone who reads the Gospels underline what appears altogether simple, clear, and understandable; let him take a pencil, a red pencil, and note the words of Christ himself, distinct from the words of the Gospel writers, and then reread those places marked in red several times. . . . Then let him reread those places that were not understandable to him, . . . that were not the words of Christ, and let him underline in red those passages which have become understandable to him. . . . The places thus marked in red will provide the reader with the essence of Christ's teaching; they will provide the reader with what all people need" (7). Perhaps the most questionable premises behind this method are the assumptions that the authors of the Gospels were not in fact the authors of the words they attribute to Jesus, and that a text may contain a reported discourse that is unrelated to the discourse in which it is couched. The fact that Tolstoy adopts such premises makes it all the more clear that he does indeed impose his own, independent outlook on the text he is examining. The reasoning that underlies this method, as he explains it in *How to Read the Gospels,* is this: "Suddenly God came to the earth for the sole purpose of saving people, and this God did not know how to say what He had to say so that people would not misinterpret His words and differ in their understanding of them. This cannot be the case if Christ was God. It cannot be the case if Christ was a great teacher, and not God. . . . So I read the Gospels and found in them a truth completely accessible even to the slow-witted, as it is said in the Gospels" (4–5). Tolstoy goes on to insist that "in order to understand the Christian teaching as it stands in reality, one must not interpret the Gospels but understand them as they are written" (5)—a rather striking statement, given the extent of his own interpretation and expurgation.

We see, then, that Tolstoy's highlighted reading of the Gospels does more than underline—it places under erasure all that requires interpretation, for interpretation is an invitation to the imposition of outside authority; his own interpretation, in short, is an anti-interpretation, an effort at the accommodation of a scriptural discourse to his own discourse. Implicit to this approach and significant to our own reading of the Gospel according to Tolstoy is the position that the capacity for understanding the truth belongs to any human

being's inherent power of reasoning; this definitive feature of
the human being is precisely what the Church would deny
through its insistence either on its unassailable authority or
on the acquiescence of faith, as Jung suggests. An important
feature of Tolstoy's theological thinking, then, is this accent
on the accessibility of the word to the human individual. He
rejects the claim of dogma that truth and the salvation it
brings must arise from an authority external to the human
being; therefore he lays out the dogmatic Russian Orthodox
text in order to eliminate it and the Greek text in order to
retrieve it through his own translation. The significance of
Christ, in Tolstoy's view, is that he reveals that divine presence within each of us by which we may overcome death, and
it is the voice of that presence that Tolstoy would make heard
in his translation. The portion of the text that Tolstoy places
under erasure lies outside of this teaching and belongs to the
externals of miracle, mystery, and authority, by which dogma
would enslave and thus destroy the soul. What remains of the
text is simply what the reasoning human being may find
within himself; to read the "genuine" word of the Gospel is to
read the text of oneself, which arises not from the page
outside the man but from the soul within him. The Gospel
according to Tolstoy—as he understands it—is therefore a
voicing not only of the truth hidden in the Greek text but of
the human soul itself. This is the text he places before his
reader, not only in his religious works but in certain notable
works of his fiction as well, where one finds direct quotation
of the Gospels. We have already pointed out his citation of
Saint Matthew in *Resurrection* (456–57). In a similar fashion,
Tolstoy inserts his own authoritative word through the words
of the Gospels in other works of fiction, including his last
short novel, *The Forged Coupon* (1904, 71–72), and short
stories such as "What Men Live By" (1881, 234) and "Where
Love Is There God Is Also" (1885, 272).

Hence, what we have before us is a process of reading far more complex than Tolstoy himself appears to realize. And a consideration of that process is necessary to a method of reading Tolstoy, both in his Gospel and in his citation of the Gospel in other works. One notes, for example, that Tolstoy takes the words of Jesus to lie in a realm of their own, as though the divine word may have penetrated the darkness of the writers' discourse despite themselves; after all, they too are human beings with souls that cast them in the image of the divine. To the extent that they are sincerely seeking the truth, something of the truth shines through in the words of the Teacher. The real Gospel, Tolstoy believes, is not what we hold between the covers of the New Testament but this truth that penetrates the veil of what might otherwise be regarded as a proselytizing discourse. The cluttered text that we have mistaken for the Gospels is, indeed, comprised of a multitude of voices or a confusion of tongues, each overlaying and interfering with the other, and not a single, authoritative, divinely inspired voice. "I am Legion, for we are many," the text seems to cry out, and Tolstoy comes onto the scene to free the text of Jesus' teaching from those other voices that threaten to possess it. As already pointed out, for Tolstoy the key to the holy word lies in our understanding of a single word, of *logos*, as *razumenie*, which is the "understanding" that he associates with something like "love-knowledge." Gustafson insightfully observes that Tolstoy's "love-knowledge" is very close to Florensky's concept of cognition, which, Gustafson explains, "is the knower's real going forth from self and what is the same thing the known's real going into the knower, a real union of known and knower" (436). Tolstoy's method of reading the Gospel is just such a going forth, and it requires a similar going forth on the part of those of us who would read him. For this Russian author, the task he undertakes in his translation of the Gospel is a matter of the greatest urgency, a matter of life and death for his own soul. Without a sense of that urgency, we can never hope to understand him.

It turns out, therefore, that Tolstoy goes beyond a simple-minded, biased process of reading certain prejudices into a text; drawing from the depths of ultimate concern, he responds to the text with an offering up of his soul and self—an offering up of his word—to the word he seeks in the text. In this union of the knower and the known, we have an instance of work and world in interaction with each other, as Bakhtin explains it in *The Dialogic Imagination:* "The work and the world represented in it enter the real world and enrich it, and the real world enters the work and its world as part of the process of its creation, as well as part of its subsequent life, in a continual renewing of the work through the creative percep-tion of listeners and readers" (254). Tolstoy's reading of the Gospels belongs to the life of the Gospels, as does our reading of Tolstoy. More than a translation and interpretation, the Gospel according to Tolstoy is a response to the voice that summons him from within and from beyond. It is a case of *logos* answering *logos,* and as such it implicates the reader in his or her responsive reading of Tolstoy. We have before us a thinker whose life is a comment on his works, not the other way around, and whose life is therefore at stake in his works. Filled with controversy, the Gospel according to Tolstoy is not a comfortable book to read precisely because it does throw us back on ourselves, on our traditions, and on our methods of reading and understanding.

Works Cited

Bakhtin, Mikhail. *The Dialogic Imagination*. Trans. Caryl Emerson and Michael Holquist. Austin: University of Texas Press, 1981.

————. *Estetika slovesnogo tvorchestva* (*The Aesthetics of Verbal Art*). Moscow: Art, 1979.

————. *Problems of Dostoevsky's Poetics*. Trans. Caryl Emerson. Minneapolis: University of Minnesota Press, 1984.

Buber, Martin. *I and Thou*. Trans. Walter Kaufmann. New York: Charles Scribner's Sons, 1970.

Gustafson, Richard F. *Leo Tolstoy: Resident and Stranger—A Study in Fiction and Theology*. Princeton, N.J.: Princeton University Press, 1986.

Jung, Carl. *Psychology and Religion*. New Haven, Conn.: Yale University Press, 1938.

Redston, David. "Tolstoy and the Greek Gospel," *Journal of Russian Studies* 54 (1988): 21–33.

Tal'berg, N. *Istoriya Russkoi Tserkvi* (*History of the Russian Church*). Jordanville, N.Y.: Holy Trinity Monastery, 1959.

Tillich, Paul. *Dynamics of Faith*. New York: Harper, 1957.

Tolstoy Leo. *Anna Karenina*. In *Sobranie sochinenii* (*Collected Works*), vol. 8–9. Moscow: Khudozhestvennaya literatura, 1981–82.

————. "Chem lyudi zhivi" ("What Men Live By"). In *Sobranie sochinenii*, vol. 10, 234–53. Moscow: Khudozhestvennaya literatura, 1982.

————. *Confession*. Trans. David Patterson. New York: W. W. Norton, 1983.

————. *The Forged Coupon*. Trans. David Patterson. New York: W. W. Norton, 1985.

————. "Gde lyubov', tam i Bog" ("Where Love Is, There God Is Also"). In *Sobranie sochinenii*, vol. 10, 262–72. Moscow: Khudozhestvennaya literature, 1984.

————. *Kak chitat' Evangelie* (*How to Read the Gospel*). 3rd ed. Essex, England: Svobodnago Slova, 1900.

————. *Kritika dogmaticheskogo bogosloviya* (*A Critique of Dogmatic Theology*). In *Polnoe sobranie sochinenii zapreshchennykh v Rossii* (*Complete Collected Works Forbidden in Russia*), vol. 2. Christchurch, England: Izdanie "Svobodnago Slova," 1903.

————. *Mysli o Boge* (*Thoughts on God*). 2nd ed. Berlin: Izdanie Hugo Steinits, 1901.

————. *O razume, vere i molitve* (*On Reason, Faith, and Prayer*). Christchurch, England: Izdanie "Svobodnago Slova," 1901.

————. *Otets Sergii* (*Father Sergius*). In *Povesti i rasskazy* (*Tales and Short Stories*), 305–47. Moscow: Sovetskaya Rossiya, 1982.

————. *Ponyatie o Boge* (*The Concept of God*). Geneva: M. Elpidine, 1897.

————. *Smert' Ivana Il'icha* (*The Death of Ivan Il'ich*). In *Povesti i rasskazy*, 176–230. Moscow: Sovetskaya Rossiya, 1982.

————. *Soedinenie, perevod i izsledovanie chetyrekh Evangelii* (*A Harmony, Translation, and Investigation of the Four Gospels*). In *Polnoe sobranie sochinenii zapreshchennykh v Rossii*, vol. 3. Christchurch, England: Izdanie "Svobodnago Slova," 1906.

————. *Tolstoy's Diaries*. Ed. and trans. R. F. Christian. Vol. 2. London: Athlone, 1985.

————. *Tolstoy's Letters*. Ed. and trans. R. F. Christian. Vol. 2. New York: Charles Scribner's Sons, 1978.

————. *Tsarstvo Bozhie vnutri vas* (*The Kingdom of God Is within You*). Geneva: M. Elpidine, 1895.

————. *Voskresenie* (*Resurrection*). In *Sobranie sochinenii*, vol. 13. Moscow: Khudozhestvennaya literatura, 1983.

The Gospel According to Tolstoy

Preface to the First Edition

Y FRIENDS have suggested that I publish this unification and translation of the Gospel that I put together ten years ago, and I have agreed in spite of the fact that this work is far from complete and contains many defects. For I feel I no longer have the strength to correct and complete it, since the concentrated, incessantly enthusiastic mental effort that I summoned in the course of this long work can no longer be renewed.

But I think that even such as it is, this work can be of use to people, if there may be imparted to them at least a small portion of the enlightenment that I experienced at the time and of the firm conviction in the truth of the way revealed to me. For the farther I go along that path, the greater is my joy.

LEO TOLSTOY
Yasnaya Polyana
29 August 1891

1

Preface to the "Free Word" Edition

I WROTE THIS BOOK at a time of unforgettable rapture in the realization that the Christian teaching expressed in the Gospels is not the strange teaching that tormented me with its contradictions and that is taught by the Church but is rather a clear, profound, and simple teaching of life that answers the highest needs of the human soul.

Unfortunately, under the influence of this rapture and enthusiasm, I did not restrict myself to presenting the intelligible portions of the Gospel that sets forth this teaching (omitting what was not consistent with and did not support or reflect the fundamental and primary meaning), but I also tried to give the obscure portions a significance supporting the general meaning. These attempts led me to artificial and probably incorrect philological explanations, which not only fail to strengthen the cogency of the general meaning but must also weaken it. Having seen the error (in addition to the fact that I was totally absorbed in other works along the same lines), I decided not to rewrite my work again, separating the superfluous from the necessary, since I knew that the work of commentaries on that amazing volume of the four Gospels could never be finished. So I have left the book as it is, and now I present it for publication in the same form.

Those people to whom the truth is dear and who sincerely seek the truth without prejudice will themselves know how to separate the superfluous from the essential without violating the essence of the content. But for people who are prejudiced, having decided beforehand that the truth lies only in the Church's interpretation, no degree of precision and clarity of account can be convincing.

LEO TOLSTOY
Koreiz
26 March 1902

Foreword

RIVEN BY REASON without faith to despair and negation of life, I was convinced after looking around at living humanity that this despair was not the common lot of people but that people had lived and continued to live through faith.

All around me I saw people who had this faith and who derived from it a meaning of life that gave them the strength to live as well as to die peacefully and joyfully. I was unable to explain that meaning to myself through reason. I tried to arrange my life like the lives of the believers; I tried to blend with them, to do everything they were doing in life, even in outward religious observance, thinking that in this way the meaning of life would be revealed to me. The closer I came to the people and the more I lived as they did, performing all the external rites of worship, the more I felt two opposing forces acting on me. On the one hand, there was revealed to me more and more a meaning of life that satisfied me and that was not destroyed by death; on the other hand, I saw a great deal of falsehood in the outward confession of faith and worship. I understood that the people could not see this lie because of ignorance, lack of time, and unwillingness to think and that I could not help but see the lie and, having seen it, could not close my eyes to it, as educated people who were believers advised me to do. The longer I continued to live, fulfilling the obligations of a believer, the more the lie bored into my eyes and demanded an investigation of where the lie ends and the truth begins in this teaching. I no longer doubted that within the Christian teaching was the very truth of life. My inner turmoil finally reached the point where I could no longer close my eyes, as I had done before, and I inevitably had to examine the doctrine that I wanted to make my own.

At first, I sought explanations from priests, monks, bishops, metropolitans, and learned theologians. All the vague passages, often unreliable, still more often contradictory, were explained; everyone cited the holy fathers, the catechisms, and theology. And I took up the theological texts and began to study them. That study led me to the conviction that the faith that our hierarchy confessed and taught to the people was not only a lie but also an immoral deception. In the Orthodox doctrine, I found a statement of the most unintelligible, blasphemous, and immoral propositions not only unacceptable to reason but completely incomprehensible and contrary to morality—and in no way a teaching on life and its meaning. I could not help seeing that theology's position was clearly directed not toward an expression of life's meaning and a teaching on life but only toward a confirmation of the propositions most incomprehensible and useless to me and a denial of all who did not acknowledge those propositions. This position directed toward the denial of other teachings automatically forced me to turn my attention to these other doctrines. The other doctrines being disputed turned out to be the same as the Orthodox doctrine that disputed them. Some more absurd, others less absurd, but all equally made assertions incomprehensible and useless for life, and in their own name, they denied each other and violated the unity of people—*the chief foundation of the Christian teaching.*

I was driven to the conviction that there was no Church at all. All the Christians with different beliefs deem themselves the true Christians and deny each other. All these separate assemblies of Christians deem themselves exclusively the Church and assure us that theirs is the true Church, that the others have broken off and fallen from it while it alone has endured. All the believers of various doctrines fail to see that their faith is true, not because it has remained thus or so but because they have been born into it or have chosen it, and that others say exactly the same thing about their own faith. Thus it is obvious that there is not now nor has there ever been a single Church, that there is not one Church or two but a thousand and two, and that they all deny one another and assert only that the one true Church is their own. Everyone says the same thing: "Ours is the true, holy, catholic, apostolic, universal Church. Ours is the Holy Scripture, the Holy Tradition; Jesus Christ is the head of our Church, which is guided by the Holy Ghost; only our Church comes by succession from Christ God."

If one takes a twig from a thick bush, it will be quite correct to say that, from twig to twig, twig to branch, and branch to root, each shoot originates from the trunk but none of them originates exclusively. They are all equal. To say that one twig is the only genuine twig would be absurd: yet this is precisely what all the churches say.

Indeed, there are a thousand traditions, and each one denies and damns the other and considers its own the true one: Catholics, Lutherans, Protestants, Calvinists, Shakers, Mormons, Greek Orthodox, Old Believers, Papists, Nonpapists, Molokans, Mennonites, Baptists, Skoptsy, Doukhobors, and on and on, all equally assert that their own faith is the only true faith and that in it alone is the Holy Ghost, that its head is Christ, and that all the others are in error. A thousand faiths and each calmly considers itself alone to be holy. And all know this, and everyone confessing his to be the one true faith knows that another faith in exactly the same manner— it cuts both ways—considers itself the true one and all others heresies. Soon it will be eighteen hundred years that this self-deception has been going on, and still it continues.

In worldly affairs, people know how to discern the most clever traps and do not fall into them, but millions have lived in this deception with eyes closed for eighteen hundred years. As if by conspiracy, everyone in our European world and in America, where everything is new, repeats the same stupid deception: each confesses his own truths of faith, regarding them as the only true statements and failing to notice that the others do exactly the same.

Furthermore, long, very long ago, freethinking people subtly and intelligently ridiculed this human stupidity and clearly showed how stupid it is. They clearly proved that the whole Christian faith with all its branches became obsolete long ago, that the time for a new faith has come, and some even invented new faiths. But no one listens to them or follows them, and as of old, everyone believes in his own peculiar Christian faith: the Catholics in theirs, the Lutherans in theirs, our Raskolnik-Papists in theirs, the Nonpapists in theirs, the Mormons in theirs, the Molokans in theirs, and the Orthodox, the very ones I wanted to join, in theirs.

What does such a thing mean? Why don't people abandon this teaching? All freethinking people who reject religion and all people of other religions agree on one answer: that Christ's teaching is good and is thus dear to people, that they cannot live without it. But why have people who believe in Christ's teaching all divided themselves into various doctrines and increasingly divide, deny, and condemn each other and cannot join together in one religious belief? Again, the answer is simple and obvious.

The reason for the division of Christians is precisely the teaching about the Church, the teaching that asserts that Christ established one true Church, which, according to its essence, is holy and infallible and can and ought to teach others. Were it not for this understanding of the "Church," there could be no division among Christians.

Every Christian church, or rather creed, undoubtedly arises from the teaching of Christ himself, but that teaching gives rise to more than one creed—from it arise all the creeds. They have all grown from a single seed, and the thing that unites them, that is common to all of them, is the thing from which they have arisen, that is, the seed. And so, to truly understand Christ's teaching, one must not study it as dogma does, from branch to trunk; nor must one study the teaching in the useless manner of science and the history of religion, proceeding from its foundation and going from trunk to branches. Neither the one nor the other offers the meaning of the teaching. The meaning is given only through an understanding of the seed and of the fruit, from which they have all risen and for which they all live. They have all come from the life and the deeds of Christ, that is, the deeds of good. And only in these deeds will they all come together. The search for the meaning of life—that is, the search for a way of life, how to live—brought me in particular to faith. And once I saw the deeds of the lives of people who confessed the teaching of Christ, I clung to them. I have encountered people who confess Christ's teaching through deeds equally and indistinguishably among the Orthodox and among the dissenters of all sects, among Catholics and Lutherans; obviously, then, the general meaning of life given by Christ's teaching is derived not from the doctrines but from something different, something common to all the doctrines. I have observed good people not of one but of various doctrines, and in all of them, I have seen one and the same meaning based on the teaching of Christ. In all those different sects of Christians, I saw complete agreement regarding what was good, what was evil, and how one must live. And all these people explained this view they held through the teaching of Christ. The doctrines have been divided, but their foundation is one; therefore, the one truth lies in the foundation of all faiths. This is the truth I now want to discover. The truth of faith is not to be found in the particular interpretations of Christ's revelation, those very interpretations that have divided Christians into a thousand sects, but must be found in the very first revelation of Christ himself. This first revelation—the work of Christ himself—lies in the Gospels. And so I turned to a study of the Gospels.

I know that, according to the teaching of the Church, the meaning of the revelation lies not in a single Gospel but in the whole Scripture and tradition preserved by the Church. I assume, in the light of what has been said, that this sophism—that the Scripture serving as the basis for my interpretation is not subject to investigation because the true and holy interpretation belongs exclusively to the Church—that this sophism must not be repeated, the more so since every interpretation is destroyed by the opposite interpretation of another Church; all the holy churches deny one another. The prohibition against this reading and understanding of the Scripture is merely a sign of those sins of interpretation that the interpreting church senses about itself.

God has revealed the truth to people. I am a man, and therefore I not only have the right but am obligated to avail myself of the truth and to stand before it face to face without mediators. If God speaks in these books, then he knows the weakness of my mind and will speak to me so as not to lead me into deception. The Church's argument that the interpreta-

tion of the Scripture cannot be granted to everyone, so that
those interpreting will not go astray and break up into a large
number of doctrines, can have no meaning for me. It might
have some meaning if the doctrine of the Church were intelligible and if there were one Church and one doctrine. But
when the Church's interpretation concerning the Son of God
and God, God in three personages, the virgin who gave birth
without damage to her virginity, the body and the blood of
God eaten in the form of bread, and so on cannot be accom-
modated by a sound mind, and when there is not one doctrine
but thousands of them, this argument, no matter how many
times it is repeated, can have absolutely no meaning. Now, on
the contrary, an interpretation is needed, one on which all
might agree. And all can agree only if the interpretation is
rational. We all come together, in spite of our differences, in
that which is rational. If this revelation is truth, then, for the
sake of persuasion, it must not and cannot fear the light of
reason: it must summon that light. If this whole revelation
turns out to be nonsense, so much the better, forget about it.
God can do everything, it is true, but there is one thing he
cannot do, and that is speak nonsense. And to write a revelation that cannot be understood would be nonsense.

I call revelation that which is revealed before reason, when
reason has reached the last of its limits—the contemplation
of divine truth, that is, truth higher than reason. I call revelation that which provides an answer to the question that
cannot be resolved by reason, that drove me to despair and
suicide: what meaning does my life have? The answer must be
intelligible and must not contradict the laws of reason, as
would, for example, the assertion that an infinite number is
even or odd. The answer must not contradict reason because
I will not believe a contradictory answer, and so it must be not
only intelligible and immutable but also inevitable to reason,
just as the recognition of infinity is inevitable to him who

knows how to count. The answer must respond to my question: what meaning does my life have? If it does not answer this question, then I have no need of it. Although its essence (like the essence of God) may be incomprehensible in itself, the answer must be such that consequences resulting from it conform to my rational demands and that the meaning imparted to my life might resolve all the questions of my life. The answer must be not only rational and clear but also correct, that is, such that I may believe in it with all my soul, believe in it inevitably, as I inevitably believe in the existence of infinity.

Revelation cannot be based on faith as the Church understands it, as a trust beforehand in what I will be told. Faith is the consequence of the inevitability and truth of revelation fully satisfying reason. According to the understanding of the Church, faith is an obligation imposed upon the soul of man with threats and enticements. According to my understanding, faith is this, that the foundation upon which every action of reason is based is true. Faith is the knowledge of revelation, without which it is impossible to live and to think. Revelation is the knowledge of what cannot be attained through reason, yet it is borne by all humanity from the beginning of all things, knowledge that is hidden in infinity. Such, in my view, must be the nature of revelation that gives rise to faith; this is what I seek in the tradition surrounding Christ, and so I turn to him with the strictest rational demands.

I do not consider the Old Testament because the question does not concern the faith of the Jews but the faith of Christ, in which people find a meaning that gives them the possibility to live. The Jewish books can be interesting to us as explanations of the forms in which Christianity was expressed, but we cannot recognize a succession of faith from Adam to our time, since prior to Christ the faith of the Jews was local. The faith of the Jews, which is foreign to us, is of interest to us, as is, for example, the faith of the Brahmins. But the faith of Christ is the faith by which we live. To study the faith of the Jews in order to understand the Christian faith is like studying the condition of a candle before lighting it in order to understand the significance of the light issuing from the burning candle. The only thing that can be said is that the character or nature of the light may depend on the candle itself, just as the form of expression in the New Testament may depend on its connection with Judaism, but the light cannot be explained by the fact that it burns on this rather than that candle.

And so the mistake made by the Church, in viewing the Old Testament to be as much a divinely inspired scripture as the New Testament, is most obviously reflected in the fact that, having acknowledged this in word, the Church does not acknowledge it in deed and has fallen into serious contradictions, from which it would never escape if it were to regard common sense as an obligation for itself.

And so I omit the writings of the Old Testament, the writings revealed, as the Church puts it, in twenty-seven books. This tradition is not, in fact, expressed in twenty-seven nor in five nor in one hundred thirty-eight books, just as the revelation of God cannot be expressed in a number of pages or letters. Saying that the revelation of God is given in one hundred eighty-five pages of writing is the same as saying that the soul of such and such a man weighs five hundred pounds or that the light from a lamp measures ten bushels. The revelation has been expressed in the souls of people, and people have passed it on to one another and wrote down some of it. From everything written down, it is known that there were over a hundred gospels and epistles not adopted by the Church. The Church selected twenty-seven books and deemed them canonical. But it is obvious that some books expressed the tradition a little better, others a little worse, and there is no breakdown into grades. The Church had to draw the line somewhere in order to delineate what it acknowledged as divinely inspired. But it is clear that nowhere could this line sharply distinguish the absolute truth from absolute lie. Tradition is like a shadow from white to black or from truth to lie, and no matter where the line is drawn, the shadows would be separated where there is black. This is precisely what the Church did in distinguishing the tradition and deeming some books canonical and others apocryphal. And it is remarkable how well it did this. It made its selections so well that the latest investigations have shown that there is nothing to be added. From these investigations, it has become clear that all the best of everything known has been gathered together by the Church in the canonical books. More than that, as if to correct the inevitable mistakes made in drawing a line, the Church has accepted some traditions from apocryphal books.

Everything that could have been done was done excellently. But in this separation, the Church erred: wishing to reject more forcibly what it did not accept and to attach more weight to what it did accept, it hastily placed the seal of infallibility on everything it accepted. Everything is from the Holy Spirit, and every word is true. In doing this, it damaged and destroyed everything it had accepted. Having accepted the white, the bright, and the gray of tradition—that is, the more or less pure teaching—and then imposing the seal of infallibility on everything, it deprived itself of the right to combine, exclude, and explain what was accepted, a duty that it did not and does not perform. Everything is sacred: the miracles, the Acts of the Apostles, Paul's advice on wine, the delirium of Revelations, and so on. Thus, existing for over eighteen hundred years, the books lie before us in the same crude, incoherent, completely absurd, contradictory form they have always been in. Having assumed that every word of the Scripture is sacred truth, the Church has tried to remove, clarify, untangle the contradictions and understand them. And it did everything it could do in this regard; that is, it gave the greatest meaning to what was meaningless. But the first mistake was fatal. After acknowledging everything as sacred truth, they had to justify everything, close their eyes, conceal, juggle around, fall into contradictions, and, alas, speak untruth. After accepting everything in word, the Church has had to deny some books in deed. Such are the whole of Revelations and portions of the Acts of the Apostles, which often not only contain nothing instructive but are actually misleading.

It is obvious that Luke wrote of miracles for the purpose of strengthening faith, and there were probably people whose faith was strengthened by this reading. But now it is impossible to find a more blasphemous book, a book more undermining to faith. Perhaps a candle is needed where there is darkness. But if there is light, there is no need to illuminate it with a candle: it will be seen as it is. The miracles of Christ are the candles brought to the light in order to illuminate it. If there is light, it will be seen as it is; if there is no light, then only the candle introduced will shine.

And so you must not and need not read the twenty-seven books in succession, acknowledging every word to be true, as the Church does, for you will arrive at exactly the same point where the Church has arrived, that is, at the point of self-negation. In order to understand the content of the Scripture that belongs to the Christian faith, we must first resolve the question of which of the twenty-seven books passed off as Holy Scripture are more or less essential and important and then begin with the more important ones. The four Gospels are undoubtedly such books. Everything preceding them may to a large extent be merely historical material for understanding the Gospel; everything that follows is merely an explanation of these books. Therefore, it is not necessary to see to it, as the churches do, that all the books agree (we are convinced that this above all has led the churches to the preaching of the incomprehensible), but it is necessary to seek in these four— which, according to the teaching of the Church, set forth the most essential material—the most central foundations of the teaching without conforming to any teaching in the other books. This is not because I do not want to conform, but because I fear the errors of the other books, which are such glaring and obvious examples of error.

In these four books I shall seek:

1. That which is comprehensible to me, because no one can believe the incomprehensible, and knowledge of the incomprehensible is the same as ignorance.
2. That which answers my question concerning what I am and what God is.
3. That which is the one primary basis of all revelation.

And so I shall read the incomprehensible, vague, half-intelligible portions, not as it suits me, but so that they may be most in agreement with the clear portions and made to conform with a single principle.

Thus, reading the Scripture and its subject matter not once or twice but many times, I came to the conclusion that the entire Christian tradition lies in the four Gospels; that the books of the Old Testament can serve only as an explanation of the form that Christ's teaching has taken, and that they can only obscure but in no way explain the meaning of Christ's teaching; that the epistles of John and James are private interpretations of the teaching occasioned by the peculiarity of the situation; and that in them it is possible to find Christ's teaching expressed from a new perspective but impossible to find anything new in itself. Unfortunately, it is

very often possible, especially in the epistles of Paul, to find
an expression of the teaching that can lead readers to misun-
derstandings that obscure the teaching itself. And the Acts of
the Apostles, like many of Paul's epistles, often not only have
nothing in common with the Gospels and the epistles of John,
Peter, and James, but even contradict them. The Book of
Revelations reveals absolutely nothing. The main point is
that, regardless of the different times when they were written, the Gospels constitute a statement of the entire teaching; everything else is merely an interpretation of them.

I read the Gospels in Greek, in the language in which we
have them, and translated them as the sense and the lexicons
indicated, now and then departing from the translations existing in modern languages and which were put together after
the Church had already understood and defined the meaning
of the tradition in its own way. In addition to translating, I
was inevitably led to the necessity of making the four Gospels
into one, since, in various ways, they give an account of the
same events and the same teaching.

The new claim of exegetes that the Gospel of John is purely
theological and ought to be considered separately has no
meaning for me, since my purpose is not historical, philosophical, or theological criticism but lies in the search for the
meaning of the teaching. The meaning of the teaching is
expressed in all four of the Gospels; therefore, if all four are
an expression of one and the same revelation of truth, then
one ought to confirm and clarify the other. And so I examined
them, combining all the Gospels into one, without excluding
the Gospel of John.

There have been many attempts to combine the Gospels
into one, but all those I know of—Arnolde de Vence, Farrar,
Reuss, Grechulevich—all unify them on a historical basis,
and all are unsuccessful. None is better than the other in a
historical sense, and all are equally satisfactory with respect

to the teaching. The advantage of unifying the Gospels as I propose is that the true teaching is a kind of circle whose parts equally define each other's meaning and which can be studied regardless of where one begins. Since the historical events in the life of Christ are so closely connected with his teaching in the Gospels studied, I was completely indifferent to the historical sequence, and it did not matter which compilation of the Gospels I selected as a basis for the order of historical events. I chose the two most recent compilations by authors who took advantage of the labors of all their predecessors: Grechulevich and Reuss. But since Reuss separates John from the Synoptics, Grechulevich's edition was more convenient for me; I took it as a basis for my work, collated it with Reuss, and departed from both whenever the meaning so demanded.

Introduction

THE ANNOUNCEMENT OF
THE BLESSEDNESS OF
JESUS CHRIST SON OF GOD

HIS ANNOUNCEMENT is recorded in order that people may believe Jesus Christ is the Son of God and that they may receive life through faith in what he was (John 20:31).

No one has ever known nor will ever know God. All that we know of God we know because we have the enlightenment.* And so the true beginning of all things is the enlightenment. (What we call God is the enlightenment. The enlightenment is the beginning of all things—it is the true God [John 1:1–2].)

Without the enlightenment, nothing can have being: all things arose from the enlightenment. In the enlightenment lies the force of life. Just as all diversity of things exists for us only because there is light, so does the diversity of life—life itself—exist for us only because there is the enlightenment. The enlightenment is the beginning of all things (John 1:3–4).

---

*Tolstoy translates the Greek word *logos* as *razumenie*, which means understanding or comprehension; I have translated *razumenie* as *enlightenment*, to suggest spiritual understanding and insight.—Translator.

In the world, life does not encompass everything. In the world, life appears like a light in the midst of darkness. The light shines while it shines, and the darkness does not suppress the light but remains darkness. Thus, in the world, life appears in the midst of death, and death does not suppress life but remains death (John 1:5).

The source of life—the enlightenment—was in all the world and in every living being. But living people—living only because the enlightenment was in them—did not realize that they arose from the enlightenment (John 1:9–10). They did not realize that the enlightenment offered them the possibility to merge with him, since their life came not from the flesh but from the enlightenment. Once they realized this and believed they were the sons of the enlightenment, people may have had life (John 1:12–13).

But people did not realize this, and life in the world was like a light in darkness. No one has ever known nor will ever know God, the beginning of all beginnings; only life in the enlightenment has shown the way to him (John 1:18).

And so Jesus Christ, living among us, evinced the enlightenment in the flesh, inasmuch as life arose from the enlightenment and is one with it, just as the Son came from the Father and is one with him. And looking upon Jesus' life, we have understood the full teaching of godliness through deeds, for because of his perfection we have realized a new godliness in place of the old. The law was given by Moses, but godliness through deeds has arisen by the life of Jesus Christ.

No one has ever seen nor will ever see God; only the Son of God in man has shown the way to him.

Chapter One

JESUS CHRIST'S BIRTH AND CHILDHOOD

AND THE BEGINNING OF

HIS PREACHING

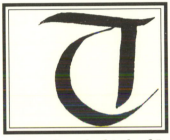 HE ENLIGHTENMENT was incarnated in Jesus Christ. Jesus Christ announced true blessedness to people.

Regarding the birth of Jesus Christ, his mother Mary was betrothed to Joseph. But before they began to live as husband and wife, Mary came to be with child.

But Joseph was a good man and did not want to cast shame upon her, so he took her to be his wife. And he had no relations with her until she bore her first son and named him Jesus.

The boy grew and reached manhood and was wise beyond his years. And this is what happened to him in his childhood:

When Jesus was twelve years old, Mary and Joseph went to Jerusalem for a holiday and took the boy with them. When the holiday was over, they set out for home but did not look after the child. Then they remembered and thought that he had gone off with some boys, and they asked about him along the road. The child was nowhere to be found, and they returned to Jerusalem to look for him.

Not until the third day did they find the boy in the temple

sitting with the teachers, asking them questions and listening. And everyone was amazed at his intelligence.

His mother saw him and said: "What have you done to us? Your father and I have been worried about you; we've been looking for you." And he said to them: "Where have you been looking for me? Don't you know that one must look for the son in the house of his father?" And they did not understand him.

They did not understand that since he had no carnal father, he considered God his only father. After that Jesus lived with his mother and obeyed her in all things. And he grew in stature and in mind and was in the good graces of God and men.

And so he lived until he was thirty years old. And everyone thought that Jesus was the son of Joseph.

This is how Jesus began to announce the good. The prophets foretold that God was to come into the world. The prophet Malachi said: "My messenger will come before me in order to prepare the way for me."

The prophet Isaiah said: "A voice calls out to you: Make a path for God into distant places, pave the way for him; make everything level, that there may be neither hollows nor hills, nothing high or low. Then God will be among you, and you will find your salvation."

According to these words of the prophets, the new prophet John appeared in the time of Jesus Christ. John lived in the plains of Judea on the Jordon. John's clothing was made of camel hair, girded with a thong. And he lived on tree bark and herbs. He summoned people to a new life; they confessed to him their wrongs, and he bathed them in the Jordon as a sign of the rectification of their wrongs. He said to all: "Have you not understood that you cannot forsake the will of God? Then be renewed. And if you want to be renewed, then let it be apparent by your deeds that you have changed." John said: "Until now the prophets have said that God will come. I say unto you, renew yourselves, for God has already come." He said: "I purify you with water, but after me, he who is mightier than I will purify you with spirit. When he comes, he will cleanse you as a master cleans his threshing floor: the wheat he will gather, but the chaff he will burn. If the tree does not bear good fruit, it is cut down and burned for firewood. And already the ax lies at the root of the tree."

And the people asked him: "What are we to do?" He answered: "He who has two coats, let him give one to him who has none. He who has food, let him share with him who has none." The tax collectors came to him and asked: "What are we to do?" He said: "Exact nothing contrary to what is proscribed." And the soldiers asked: "How are we to act?" He said: "Harm no one. Do not cheat. Be satisfied with what is allotted to you." And much more he proclaimed to the people concerning what genuine blessedness is.

At that time, Jesus was thirty years old. He came to John at the Jordon and listened to his preaching about the coming of God, about the need to be renewed, and about the purification of people with water, that they must be purified with spirit before God will come. Jesus did not know his carnal father and considered God his father. He believed in John's preaching and said to himself: "If it is true that God is my father and I am the Son of God, and if what John says is true, then I need only be purified by the spirit in order that God may come to me."

And Jesus departed into the wilderness to test the truth that he was the Son of God and that God would come to him. He departed into the wilderness and without food or drink lived there a long time and finally became emaciated. And doubt came over him, and he said to himself: "You say you are spirit, the Son of God, and that God will come to you, and yet you are tormented because you have no bread and God does not come to you; hence you are not spirit, not the Son of

God." But he said to himself: "My flesh longs for bread, but I do not need bread for life; man lives not by bread but by the spirit—by that which is from God." But hunger continued to torment him.

Another doubt came over him, and he said to himself: "You say you are the Son of God and that God will come to you, yet you suffer and cannot bring your sufferings to an end." And he imagined that he was standing on the roof of the temple, and a thought came to him: "If I am spirit, the Son of God, then I may cast myself from the temple and I will not be killed, but an invisible force will preserve and support me and deliver me from all evil. Why should I not cast myself down to stop suffering from hunger?" But he said to himself: "Why should I test God to see whether he is with me? If I test him, I do not believe in him, and he is not with me. God the spirit gives me life, and so in life the spirit is always within me. And I cannot test it. I may not eat, but I cannot kill myself because I feel the spirit within me." But hunger continued to torment him.

And still another thought came to him: "If I must not test God by throwing myself from the temple, then I also must not test God by going hungry when I want to eat. I must not deprive myself of all the lusts of the flesh. They lie within me and within all people." And he imagined all the kingdoms of the earth and all the people, how they lived and labored for the flesh, expecting rewards for their efforts. And he thought: "They work for the flesh, and it gives them everything they have. If I work for the flesh, it will do the same for me." But he said to himself: "My God is not flesh but spirit; I live by him, within myself I know him always, him alone I hold sacred. And for him alone I labor, from him alone I expect rewards."

Then the temptation left him and the spirit renewed him, and he knew that God had come to him and would always be within him. Realizing this, he returned to Gailee in the power of the spirit.

And from that time, having realized the power of the spirit, he began to proclaim the presence of God. He said: "The time has come. Renew yourself, believe in the announcement of blessedness."

From out of the wilderness, Jesus came again to John and was with him.

When Jesus left, John said of him: "This is the true Son of God" (the chosen one). Upon hearing these words, two of John's disciples left their former teacher and followed Jesus.

Jesus saw that they were following him, stopped, and said: "What do you want?" They said to him: "Teacher, we want to be with you and learn your teaching." He said: "Come with me, and I will tell you everything." They went with him and stayed with him, listening to him the whole day until the tenth hour.

One of these disciples was called Andrew. And Andrew had a brother named Simon. After listening to Jesus, Andrew went to his brother Simon and said to him: "We have found the chosen one of God." Andrew took Simon with him and brought him to Jesus. This brother of Andrew Jesus called Peter, which means "the rock." And both brothers became disciples of Jesus.

And Jesus walked on with his two disciples. After going a short way, Jesus saw some fishermen in a boat. They were the father Zebedee with some servants and his two sons Jacob and John. They were sitting and mending their nets. Jesus began to speak with Jacob and John, and Jacob and John left their father with the servants in the boat and went with Jesus and became his disciples.

Then, just before entering Galilee, Jesus met Philip and called him to come with him. Philip was from Bethsaida, the same village Peter and Andrew were from. When Philip recognized Jesus, he went and told his brother Nathaniel and said to him: "We have found the chosen one of God, the one of whom Moses wrote; it is Jesus, the son of Joseph of Nazareth." Nathaniel was surprised that the chosen one of God was from a neighboring village and said: "Well, brother, it is strange that the chosen one of God should be from Nazareth." Philip said: "Go to him with me, and you will see and hear for yourself." Nathaniel agreed and went with his brother and met Jesus. And when he had heard him, he said to Jesus: "Yes, now I see that it is true. You are the Son of God and the King of Israel."

Jesus said to him: "You will discover what is more important than this. You will discover that the new kingdom of heaven has come, and so I tell you truly that the power of God will descend upon all people, and from them will emanate the power of God. From this day, God will no longer be isolated from people, but people will merge with God."

And from out of the wilderness, Jesus came to his home in Nazareth. And on a certain holiday, as always, he entered the assembly and began to read. He was given the book of the prophet Isaiah. He unrolled it and began to read. In the book it was written: "The spirit of the Lord is within me. He has chosen me to proclaim blessedness to the unfortunate and broken-hearted; to proclaim freedom to the enslaved, light to the blind, salvation and rest to the weary; to announce to all the time of salvation and the mercy of God." He closed the book, gave it to a servant, and sat down. All awaited what he would say. And he said: "This Scripture has now been fulfilled before your eyes. God is in the world. The kingdom of God has come, and all the unfortunate, the broken-hearted, the enslaved, the blind, the weary—all will receive salvation."

And many were amazed at the goodness of his speech. But others said: "He is a carpenter, you know, and the son of carpenters. And his mother's name is Mary, and his brothers are James, Simon, Jude, and Joset, and we all know them. They are all as poor as we are."

And he said to them: "I am sure you are thinking, from what I say, that there are no more of the unfortunate or weary; that I have a mother, father, and brothers who are poor; that I am speaking an untruth; and that I must make them all happy. If you think this way, then you do not understand what I am saying. And so a prophet is never understood in his homeland."

And Jesus went to Capernaum and on the Sabbath entered the assembly and began to teach. And all the people marveled at his teaching, because his teaching was completely different from the teaching of those versed in the law. Those versed in the law taught the law, which must be obeyed, but Jesus taught that all people were free.

Chapter Two

THE NEW WORSHIP OF GOD
IN SPIRIT THROUGH DEEDS.
THE REJECTION OF THE JEWISH GOD

 *ND JESUS SHOWED all people that the former worship of God was a lie and that God must be served by deeds and compassion toward people.*

He happened to walk across a field with his disciples on the Sabbath. Along the way, his disciples picked some ears of corn, rubbed them in their hands, and ate.

Some of those versed in the law, Pharisees, saw this and said: "One ought not do this on the Sabbath." Jesus heard and said to them: "If you understood the meaning of what God said to the prophet—'I rejoice in the love of people for one another and not in sacrifices that they bring to me'—then you would not condemn the innocent. Indeed, the Sabbath was established not by God but by man, and so man is more important than the Sabbath."

It happened another time on the Sabbath, when Jesus was teaching in the assembly, that a sick woman came up to him and asked him to help her. And Jesus began to treat her. And one of those versed in the law, an elder in the assembly, became angry at Jesus and said to the people: "In God's law it is written: 'There are six days in the week for working. But on the Sabbath, God commands us not to work.'" And at that, Jesus asked the ones versed in the law and the Pharisees: "Do you mean to say that it is not permitted to help a man on the Sabbath?"

And they did not know what to answer.

Then Jesus said: "Does not each of you untie his cattle from their stalls and lead them to drink on the Sabbath? Or if one of your sheep should fall into a well, any of you would certainly run quickly to pull it out, even on the Sabbath. Yet you say it is not permitted to help a man. What, then, according to you, is to be done on the Sabbath: good or evil? Is it to save the soul or to perish? One must always do good—even on the Sabbath."

Pharisees and men versed in the law came to Jesus from Jerusalem. And they saw that he and his disciples were eating bread together with unwashed hands. And those versed in the law began to condemn him for it, because they themselves acted strictly, according to the old ways. They washed their plates, and if their hands were not washed, they would not eat, and when they returned from the market, they would not begin to eat without washing their hands. And one versed in the law asked him: "Why do you not act according to the old ways, taking and eating bread with unwashed hands?" And he said to them: "Truly the prophet Isaiah spoke of you. God said to him: 'Because these people cling to me only in words and worship me only with their tongues, their hearts are far from me. And because their fear before me is only a human commandment that they have memorized, I shall perform an amazing, extraordinary work over these people. And the wisdom of their wise will vanish, and the reason of their intellectuals will dim.' Woe to those who struggle to hide their desires from the Eternal One and who do their deeds in darkness. So do you abandon what is vital in the law, that which is the commandment of God, and observe your own injunctions—to wash cups. Moses has said to you: 'Honor your father and your mother, and he who does not honor father and mother shall be put to death.' But you have made up what anyone can say: you give to God what your parents gave—and then you fail to provide for your father and mother. Thus, with human resolutions, you destroy the commandment of God. And you do many such things."

Jesus summoned all the people and said: "Listen, all of you, and understand: there is nothing in the world that could defile a man by entering him. But that which comes out of a man is what defiles him. Let there be love and mercy in your soul, and then all will be pure. Try to understand this."

And when he returned home, his disciples asked him what these words meant. And he said: "Can it be that you too have not understood? Do you really not understand that nothing external and carnal can debase a man, because it enters not his soul but his belly? It enters the belly and then comes out the back. Only what comes out of the man, out of his soul, can debase him. For evil proceeds from the soul of man: lechery, obscenity, murder, thievery, greed, malice, deception, insolence, envy, slander, pride, every folly. All this evil comes from the soul, and it alone can defile a human being."

Jesus taught that a new life had begun and that God is in the world, on earth, and this he told to everyone, and he told his disciples that there is continual interaction between man and God. He taught this to all. And all were enraptured by his teaching, because he did not teach as those versed in the law did. Those versed in the law taught people that they must obey the laws of God, but he taught people that they were free.

After that, Passover approached, and Jesus went to Jerusalem and entered the temple. In the vestibule of the temple stood livestock: cattle, oxen, sheep, and baskets of doves, and

there were money changers with money set up behind coun-
ters. All this was necessary for making offerings to God. They
killed and made offerings in the temple, and they offered up
money in the temple. Among the Jews, prayer consisted of
this. Jesus entered the temple, coiled up a whip, and drove all
the livestock from the vestibule, released all the doves, and
scattered all the money. And he commanded that no one
should bring any of this into the temple.

He said: "The prophet Isaiah told you: 'The house of God
is not the temple in Jerusalem but the whole world of God's
people.' And the prophet Jeremiah also said to you: 'Do not
believe the lying speeches that here is the house of the
Eternal One, the house of the Eternal One, the house of the
Eternal One; do not believe this, but change your life; do not
judge falsely; do not oppress the stranger, the widow, and the
orphan; do not spill innocent blood; and do not come into the
house of God and say: "Now we can calmly do foul things."
Do not make my house into a den of thieves.'"

And the Jews began to argue and said to him: "If you forbid
our prayer and our image of God, what form of prayer will you
give us?"

And Jesus turned to them and said: "Cast off this temple,
and in three days, I will raise up a new, living temple to God."

And the Jews said: "How can you make a new temple all at
once, when it took forty-six years to build this one?"

And Jesus said: "I am speaking to you of what is more
important than the temple. You would not say this if you
understood what the words of the prophet mean: 'I, God, do
not rejoice in your sacrifices, but I rejoice in your love for one
another.' The living temple is the entire world of God's people
when they love one another."

And then many people in Jerusalem believed in what he
said. But he himself did not believe in anything external
because he knew of all that was within man. He did not need

anyone to teach him about man because he knew that the spirit of God was in man.

And those versed in the law and the elders heard all this and sought ways to ruin him, but they were afraid of him because all the people marveled at his teaching.

And Jesus went again from Judea to Galilee. And he had to pass through Samaria. He was walking by the Samaritan village of Sychar, near the place that Jacob had given to his son Joseph. Jacob's well was there. Jesus was worn out from the road and sat down next to the well. But his disciples went into town for bread.

And a woman came from Sychar for water. Jesus asked her for a drink. She said to him: "How is it that you ask me for a drink? You know you Jews do not associate with us Samaritans."

But he said to her: "If you knew me and knew what I teach, you would not say that but would offer me a drink, and I would give you living water. He who drinks his fill of this water will want to drink yet again, but he who drinks his fill of my water will be satisfied forever, and my water will lead him to life eternal."

The woman realized that he was speaking of the divine and said to him: "I see that you are a prophet, and I want you to teach me, but how can you teach me about the divine when you are a Jew and I am a Samaritan? Our people pray to God on this mountain, while you Jews say that one must pray in Jerusalem. You cannot teach me about the divine because you have one God, and we have another."

Jesus said to her: "Believe me, woman, the time is drawing near when people will pray to the Father neither on this mountain nor in Jerusalem. You pray to one whom you do not know, but we pray to the Father, to the one whom it is impossible not to know. The time has been coming, and now it has come, when the real worshipers of God will worship the Father in spirit and in deed. The Father needs such worshipers. God is spirit, and he must be worshiped in spirit and in deed."

The woman could not make out what he said to her and replied: "I have heard that a messenger of God would come, he who is called the Anointed One. When he comes he will tell all."

And Jesus said to her: "I who am speaking to you am that very one. Await no one else."

After that Jesus came into the land of Judea and taught there while living with his disciples.

At that time, John was purifying people in the river Enon near Salem, for John had not yet been thrown into prison. And an argument arose between the disciples of John and the disciples of Jesus about which was better—John's purification by water or the teachings of Jesus. And they came to John and said to him: "You purify with water, while Jesus simply teaches, and everyone is going to him. What will you say about him?"

And John said: "Man can teach nothing of himself if God does not teach him. Whoever speaks of the earthly is of the earth, but if he speaks from God, he is from God. There is no way to prove whether the words spoken are from God. God is spirit; he cannot be measured, and he cannot be proven. He who understands the words of God proves that he has understood God."

Jesus once saw a tax collector collecting taxes. The tax collector's name was Matthew. Jesus began to speak with him, and Matthew understood him, came to love his teaching, and invited him to his home. And he provided him with entertainment. When Jesus came to Matthew's home, Matthew's friends also came—tax collectors and profligates. Jesus did not shun them but sat down with them, as did his disciples. Those versed in the law and the Pharisees saw this and said to Jesus' disciples: "How is it that your teacher feasts with tax collectors and profligates?" Jesus heard and said: "He who boasts of good health does not need a doctor, but rather he who is sick. For this reason, I do not want to convert those who consider themselves righteous and think they live by the truth, but I teach those who believe they live in sin."

And after that, a certain Pharisee came to him and invited him to breakfast. He went in and sat down at the table. The Pharisee noticed that he did not wash before breakfast and was shocked. And Jesus said to him: "Pharisee, you wash everything on the outside, but are you clean on the inside? Be kind to people, and everything will be clean."

And while he was sitting in the home of the Pharisee, there came a city woman who had led a dissolute life. She had found out that Jesus was in the home of the Pharisee and had come there and brought a vial of perfume. And she knelt at his feet, began to weep, and washed his feet with her tears. She wiped them dry with her hair and poured perfume on them from the bottle. Seeing this, the Pharisee thought to himself: "He is hardly a prophet; if he were a prophet, he would know what sort of woman was washing his feet. He would know that she is a harlot and would not let her touch him."

Jesus guessed what he was thinking, turned to him, and said: "Shall I tell you, Simon, what I am thinking?"

"Tell me," he said.

And Jesus said: "This: Two men were debtors to one master, one for five hundred denarii, the other for fifty. And neither had anything with which to pay. And the master forgave both. So, according to your judgment, which will love the master and look after him?"

And Simon said: "Why, the one who was in the greater debt, of course."

Jesus pointed to the woman and said: "So it is with you and this woman. You consider yourself a small debtor, while she considers herself a great debtor. I came to your home, and you gave me no water to wash my feet, while she has washed them with her tears and dried them with her hair. You did not kiss me, but she kisses my feet; you do not give me oil to anoint my head, but she rubs my feet with expensive perfume. Whoever thinks he has nothing to be forgiven does not love. Whoever thinks he is guilty of much loves much. And for love, all is forgiven." And he said to her: "Your sins are forgiven."

And Jesus said: "The whole matter lies in what a person considers himself to be. He who considers himself good will not be good, while he who considers himself bad is good."

And he told them a parable. Two men once came to pray in the temple. One was a Pharisee, the other a man who did not observe the law. The Pharisee prayed like this: "I thank Thee, Lord, that I am not like others; I am neither a miser nor a deceiver nor a profligate nor a scoundrel like this tax collector. I fast twice a week and give a tenth of my possessions." But the one who did not observe the law stood at a distance and did not dare to look up to heaven and just beat himself on the chest and said over and over: "Lord, look upon me, a worthless man!"

The man who did not observe the law was forgiven more than the Pharisee: for he who ennobles himself will be humbled, and he who humbles himself will be ennobled.

After this, John's disciples came to Jesus and said: "Why do we and those versed in the law fast a great deal, while you and your disciples do not fast?" And Jesus said to them: "As long as the bridegroom is at the wedding, no one mourns. Only when the bridegroom has gone is there mourning. If there is life, then one ought not mourn."

And Jesus also said: "No one tears off a piece of new clothing to sew it on old, for the new garment will be torn, and the old one will not be mended. So we must not accept your fasts. And new wine must not be poured into old wineskins, for the wineskins will be torn and the wine will run out. But new wine must be poured into new wineskins, and both will be whole."

And Jesus's fame spread, and he was revered by all. So the people tried to keep him from leaving them. But he said he had come to proclaim blessedness not to one city but to all people.

And he went farther along the coast. And many people from various cities followed him. And he helped them all. And he walked through cities and villages announcing the kingdom of God and delivering people from all suffering and vices.

Thus, in Jesus Christ were fulfilled the prophecies of Isaiah; for, having lived in darkness and in the blackness of death, the people saw the light of life. They saw that he who brought the light of truth would do no violence or harm to anyone; that he was meek and humble; that in order to bring truth to the world, he did not argue or shout; that his loud voice was not heard; that he did not break a straw or blow out a lamp; and that all the hope of the people was in him.

Chapter Three

THE KINGDOM OF GOD

ESUS ANNOUNCED that the kingdom of God had come, even though there had been no visible manifestation.

He announced to his disciples that, from now on, heaven is open and that there is constant interaction between heaven and people.

He announced that it is not necessary to be separated from profligate men and women; that they are not guilty; that the only guilty ones are those who think they are good because they fulfill the law of God.

He announced that no external purifications are necessary; that only what comes from within corrupts; that only the spirit purifies.

He announced that it is not necessary to observe the Sabbath; that the observance of it is stupid and false; that the Sabbath is a human institution.

He announced that not only is fasting unnecessary but that all the old external rituals are pernicious to his teaching.

Finally, he announced that it is not necessary to serve God with sacrifices. Neither oxen nor sheep nor doves nor money nor even the temple itself is needed; that God is spirit; that he does not want sacrifices but love; that he must be served—by everyone, always, everywhere—in spirit and in deed.

Having seen and heard all this, the Pharisees came to Jesus and began to ask him how he, in denying God, could preach the kingdom of God. And he answered them: "The kingdom of God, as I preach it, is not what the prophets of old used to preach. They said there would be various manifestations of God's coming, but I speak of a kingdom of God whose coming cannot be seen.

"And do not believe those who tell you, look, it has come or will come, or here it is. The kingdom of God is not in time or in any certain place, but like lightning, it is here and there and everywhere—it has neither time nor space, for this is where it is: it is within you."

After this, a Pharisee, the Jewish elder Nicodemus, secretly came to Jesus and said: "You teach that the kingdom of God has come and that it is within us, yet you do not order fasting or the offering of sacrifices; you have destroyed the temple. What kind of kingdom is your kingdom of God, and where is it?"

And Jesus answered him: "Understand that if a man is conceived from God the Father, then he will see the kingdom of God."

Nicodemus did not understand that Jesus was telling him that *every man is already conceived from God,* and he said: "How can a man conceived from the flesh of his father and grown old crawl back into his mother's womb and again be conceived *from the spirit—from God?*"

And Jesus answered him: "Understand what I say: I say that in addition to the flesh, man is conceived from the spirit, and so every man is of flesh and spirit; every man can enter the kingdom of God. Flesh is of the flesh. Spirit cannot be born from the flesh; only from the spirit can there be spirit.

Spirit is that which lives within you and lives freely and rationally, that which has neither beginning nor end. Every man feels this within himself. Why, then, are you surprised that I said to you that we must be conceived from heaven, from God—from spirit?"

Nicodemus said, "Still I do not believe that this could be so."

Then Jesus said to him: "What sort of teacher are you, if you do not understand this? Understand that I do not expound any kind of profundities; I expound what we all know, I attest to what we all see. How will you believe in what is in heaven, if you do not believe in what is on earth, in what is within yourself? No one has ever been in heaven, and only on earth, in man, is there the Son of God—the spirit, *the very one who is God himself.*

"It is this very Son of God in man that must be held sacred, as you have held God sacred, as Moses in the wilderness exalted not the flesh of the serpent but its image, and that image became the salvation of the people. Precisely in this way must the Son be exalted—God in man, not the flesh of man, but the Son of God in man, so that, relying on the Son, people may not know death but may have a life outside of time, in the kingdom of God.

"Not for ruin but for the blessedness of the world has God given his Son, the one who is like himself. He has given him so that, relying upon him, every person may not perish but have a life outside of time. For he did not bring his Son, who is life, into the world of people to destroy that world, but he brought his Son, who is life, so that the world of people might live through him, in the kingdom of God.

"And he who relies on the Son is in the kingdom of God, in the power of God, but he who does not rely on him destroys himself by failing to rely on that which is life. Destruction consists of this, that life has come into the world, but people themselves turn away from life. Life is the light of people. The light has come into the world, but people prefer darkness to the light and do not move toward the light. The light is the enlightenment, and so he who does evil evades the light of the enlightenment, so that his deeds may not be seen, and he departs from the kingdom of God, from the power of God.

"But he who lives in truth moves toward the light, so that his deeds may be seen, and he remains in the power of God."

In his remarks to the Pharisees and in his conversation with Nicodemus, Jesus explained what he means by "the kingdom of God" and by "God."

Both God and the kingdom of God are in people. God is the noncarnal origin or principle that gives life to man. This noncarnal principle he calls the Son of God in man, the Son of man. The Son of man is the enlightenment. He must be raised up, worshiped, and lived by. People who do evil perish; people who do what is true live. He who lives in the enlightenment lives outside of time; he who does not live in it does not live but perishes.

Who, then, is this God the Father, who is not the creator of all things, not the God separate from the world, as the Jews had conceived him? How are we to understand this Father, whose Son is in man, and how are we to understand his relation to people?

Jesus answered this in parables.

"The kingdom of God must not be understood as you think, that the kingdom of God will come for people at some time and in some place, but that in all the world there are always certain people who rely on the Son of God, who become sons of the kingdom, while there are others who do not rely on him and are destroyed."

The God-spirit, the Father of the spirit that is man, is God and Father only to those who recognize themselves to be his sons. That is why, for God, only those exist who retain in themselves what he has given them.

And Jesus began to speak to them of the kingdom of God, and he spoke of it through examples. He said:

"God the Father sows in the world the life of the enlightenment, just as a farmer plants seeds in his field. He plants the whole field without worrying which seed will fall where. And so some seeds will fall onto the road, and the birds will come and devour them. Others will fall among stones, and, although they will indeed sprout, they soon wither because they have no place to take root. And still others will fall among thorns, and the thorns will choke the wheat, and the ears will blossom but will not fill out. And others will fall on good earth, and they rise up and make up for the lost seeds; they fill out with full ears, and some ears give a hundredfold, some sixtyfold, some thirtyfold.

"Just so has God scattered the enlightenment among people. In some, it is lost, but in others, it bears a hundredfold, and they make up the kingdom of God.

"Thus, the kingdom of God is not what you think, that God will come to rule over you. God only sows the enlightenment, and the kingdom of God will be in those who accept it. But God does not govern people.

"The farmer casts his seeds to the earth and does not think about them; the seeds themselves will burst forth, sprout, grow into leaves and stalks, and fill out with grain. And only when the time has come does the farmer send the sickles to harvest the field.

"So has God given his Son, the enlightenment, to the world. And the comprehension will itself grow in the world, and the sons of the enlightenment will make up the kingdom of God.

"Just as a peasant woman empties leaven into a trough and

mixes it with flour; she no longer controls it but waits for it to leaven of itself and rise.

"God does not enter the lives of people while they live. God has given the enlightenment to the world, and the enlightenment itself lives in people and comprises the kingdom of God. The God-spirit is the God of life and of good, and so for him there is neither death nor evil. Death and evil are of people, not of God.

"The kingdom of God is to be compared to this: A farmer has sown his field with good seeds. The farmer is the spirit of God, the field is the world, and the seeds are the sons of the kingdom of God. The farmer lay down to sleep, and the enemy came and planted tares in the field. The enemy is temptation, the tares the sons of temptation. And then the workers came to the farmer and said: 'Have you sown bad seeds? Many tares have sprouted in your field. Send us out, and we will pull them up.' But the farmer says: 'It is not necessary, for when you start weeding the tares, you will trample the wheat. Let them grow together. When the harvest comes, I will order the reapers to take out the tares and burn them, and the wheat I will take to my barn.'

"The harvest is the end of human life, and the reapers are the might of God. Just as the tares will be burned and the wheat purified and gathered up, so will all that had been the deception of time perish, and only the genuine life in the spirit will remain. For God there is no evil. God watches over what he needs, over what is his; that which does not come from him does not exist for him.

"The kingdom of God is like a net. The net is cast out on the sea and catches all sorts of fish. And then, when it is pulled in, the worthless ones will be taken out and tossed back into the sea. So shall it be at the end of time. The might of God will select the good, and the bad will be cast out."

When he had finished speaking, his disciples began to ask how to understand these parables.

And he said to them: "These parables must be understood in two ways. For I speak all these parables because there are some like you, my disciples, who understand what the kingdom of God consists in; who understand that the kingdom of God is within everyone; who understand how to enter it. But others do not understand this. Others look and do not see, listen and do not understand. For their hearts have grown fat.

"And so with these parables I address two matters. To some I say what God's kingdom is to him; I speak of the fact that some enter the kingdom and others do not, and they can understand this. But I tell you how to enter the kingdom of God. And you look and understand that the parable of the sower is fitting. This is what the parable means for you:

"Anyone who listens to the teaching on the kingdom of God but does not accept it in his heart falls into deception and, from within his heart, destroys the teaching—this is the seed fallen to the wayside. As for the seed planted among stones, this is the one who hears the teaching and accepts it with joy. But there are no roots within him; he accepts it only for a time, and when he is oppressed or hurt because of the teaching, he is immediately offended. The seed sown among thorns is the one who hears the teaching, but worldly cares and greed for wealth suffocate the teaching, and it yields no fruit. The seed sown in good earth is the one who hears the teaching and understands and bears fruit, some a hundredfold, some sixtyfold, some thirtyfold. Thus, whoever holds fast will be given much, but whoever does not hold fast will lose the ultimate thing. And so you see how to understand the parables. Understand, so you will not submit to deception, offenses, and cares but will bring forth fruit a hundredfold and enter the kingdom of God.

"The kingdom of heaven grows within the soul from nothing but gives everything. Like a birch seed, it is the smallest of seeds, but when it grows up, it is the largest of trees, and the birds of the sky make their nests in it."

After this, the disciples of John came to Jesus to ask whether he was the one of whom John spoke, whether he revealed the kingdom of God and renewed people with the spirit.

Jesus answered and said: "Look, listen, and tell John whether the kingdom of God has come and whether people are renewed with the spirit. Tell him how I preach the kingdom of God. In the prophecies, it is said that when the kingdom of God comes, all people will be blessed; tell him, then, that my kingdom of God is such that beggars are blessed and that anyone who listens to me is blessed."

And upon dismissing John's disciples, Jesus explained to the people what kind of kingdom of God John proclaimed.

He said: "When you went into the wilderness to be baptized by John, what did you go to see? If you wanted to see a man dressed in rich clothes, such men live here in the palaces. What, indeed, did you see in the wilderness? Do you think you went because John was a prophet? Do not think it. John was not a prophet but was the one of whom the prophets wrote. He is the one who has proclaimed the coming of the kingdom of God. Truly I say unto you: no man greater than John has ever been born. He has been in the kingdom of God and thus has been higher than all. The law and the prophets were all necessary prior to John. But since John and from this time on, it is proclaimed that the kingdom of God is on earth, and whoever makes the effort will enter it. The Pharisees and those versed in the law have not understood what John has proclaimed. Nor have they had any regard for him. This breed—the Pharisees and those versed in the law—takes truth to be only what they themselves fabricate. They repeat their law over and over and listen only to each other. But what John has said, what I am saying, they do not hear and do not understand. From what John has said, they have understood only that he fasted in the wilderness, and they say: 'A devil is in him.' From what I say, they have understood only that I do not fast, and they say: 'He eats and drinks with tax collectors and is a friend to profligates.' Like children in the street, they chatter among themselves and marvel that no one listens to them. Their wisdom is seen by their deeds. But everything I teach you to do is easy and simple, for the kingdom of God is proclaimed as a beatitude."

Chapter Four

THE LAW

OHN ANNOUNCED the coming of God into the world. He said that people must be purified by the spirit in order to know the kingdom of God.

Not knowing his carnal father and recognizing God as his father, Jesus heard the preaching of John and asked himself, "What is this God, how has he come into the world, and where is he?"

And having gone off into the wilderness, Jesus realized that the life of man lies in the spirit, and having been convinced of this, he realized that man always lives through God, that God is always within people, and that the kingdom of God is and always has been. People have but to recognize it. Once he understood this, Jesus came out of the wilderness and began to preach to people that God is and always has been in the world and that in order to know him, one must be purified, returned to life through the spirit.

He announced that God has no need of prayers, sacrifices, or temples but requires spiritual devotion and deeds of goodness. He announced that the kingdom of God must not be understood as the coming of God at some time or place, but that in all the world, always, all people who have been purified through the spirit may live in the power of God. He announced that the kingdom of God does not come in a visible form but that it lies within people. In order to be part of the kingdom, one must be purified through the spirit; that is, one must raise up the spirit within man and serve it. He who raises up the spirit enters the kingdom of God and receives life beyond time. Every man has within himself the capacity to raise up the spirit and become part of the kingdom of God, and from the time John announced the kingdom of God, the Jewish law has become unnecessary. Anyone who has understood the kingdom of God and, by his own effort, has raised up the spirit within himself and is working for the sake of God enters into the power of God.

In order to work for God and live in his kingdom, that is, to submit to him and fulfill his will, it is necessary to know the law of that kingdom. And so Jesus announced what the elevation of the spirit and service to God ought to consist of, what the law of the kingdom of God consists of.

Jesus prayed all night, and after choosing twelve men who had fully understood him, he went out with them to the people and declared what ascent through the spirit and service to God entail; he declared where the law of the kingdom of God lies.

The law of the power of God lies above all in this, that the whole man may be given over to the power of God. And so, after gazing upon the people, Jesus pointed to his disciples and said:

"Happy are you, vagrants: you are in the power of God. You are happy: though you are hungry now and may be hungry for a time, you will be filled. You are happy: though you mourn and weep for a time, you will be comforted. You are happy: though people consider you to be nothing and drive you away from everywhere. Rejoice in this, for thus have people driven away all who have proclaimed the will of God.

"But unhappy are you who are wealthy, for you have already received all that you desired, and you will receive nothing more. If you are filled now, you will be hungry. If you are cheerful now, you will mourn. Unhappy are you if everyone praises you, for everyone praises only liars.

"Happy are you, vagrants: you are in the power of God. But you are happy when you are vagrants not merely in appearance but in your soul, just as salt is good not when it merely looks like salt but is itself salty. Just so are you the salt of the world, the teachers of the world, if you know that true happiness lies in being a vagrant. But if you are vagrants only in appearance, then, like unsalty salt, you are good for nothing. If you understand this, then show by your deeds that you desire to be vagrants, and do not be like others.

"If you are a light unto people, then show your light, and do not hide it, so that people may see that you indeed know the truth and, looking upon your deeds, may realize that you are the sons of your Father, the sons of God.

"And do not suppose that being a vagrant means being a criminal. I do not teach so that you may relinquish God's law; on the contrary, I teach so that God's law may be fulfilled. As long as there are people under heaven, there is for all a law concerning what ought and ought not to be. The law will no longer exist only when people themselves are fulfilled through themselves according to the law. And so I give you rules for the fulfillment of the law.

"And if a person should not fulfill even one of them and should teach that it need not be fulfilled, he will be the farthest from God. But he who fulfills them all and so teaches is nearest to God. For if, in your faithfulness to the fulfillment of the law, there is no more than the faithfulness of the Pharisees and the scribes, then you will not be joined with God.

"And here are the rules:

"This is the *first rule:* The justice of the scribes and Pharisees consists in this, that if one man kills another, then he must be judged and sentenced to punishment.

"But my rule is this, that being angry with one's brother is just as evil as killing. I forbid malice toward your brother under the same warning that the Pharisees and the scribes forbid murder. It is worse still to abuse your brother, and I forbid it under even greater warning; still worse is to insult your brother, and this I forbid even more severely.

"I forbid this because you think it is necessary for God's sake to go to the temple and offer sacrifices. And so you offer sacrifices. But know that, as important as you think sacrifices are, still more important are peace, harmony, and love among people for God's sake. Know that you must neither pray nor think about God if there is even a single human being whom you do not love.

"Thus, here is the first rule: Do not grow angry, do not quarrel, but when you have quarreled, be reconciled. And forgive all people who are guilty before you.

"This is the *second rule:* The Pharisees and the scribes say, 'If you commit adultery, then you and the woman are to be killed, and if you want to commit adultery, then give your wife a divorce.'

"But I say that if you abandon your wife, then not only are you a profligate but you also drive her to debauchery, as well as the one who takes up with her. If you live with your wife and consider loving another woman, you are already an adulterer and deserve having done to you what is done to an adulterer according to the law. And under the same warning that the Pharisees and the scribes forbid adultery with another man's wife, I forbid taking a woman as a lover. I forbid it because all debauchery destroys the soul; so it is better for you to renounce all pleasures of the flesh than to destroy your life.

"Thus, the second rule is: Satisfy your lust only with your wife, and do not think that love of woman is a good thing.

"This is the *third rule:* The Pharisees and the scribes say, 'Do not pronounce the name of the Lord God in vain, for God does not leave the one who pronounces his name in vain without punishment: that is, do not call upon thy God in a lie.' Furthermore, God himself says: 'Do not swear by my name to a lie, and do not dishonor the name of thy God. I am the Lord (your God); that is, do not swear by me to an untruth so as to defile your God.'

"But I say that any oath is a defilement of God, so *do not swear at all.* You most promise nothing because you are completely in the power of God. You cannot make a single gray hair black; how can you swear beforehand that you will do this or that and swear by God? Your every oath is a defilement of God, for if you should have to fulfill an oath contrary to the will of God, then it will happen that you have promised to act against his will. And so every oath is an evil. Not only that, an oath is stupidity and nonsense.

"So this is the third rule: Never swear to anything before anyone. Say yes when you mean yes, no when you mean no. And know that if an oath is demanded of you, then it is for the sake of evil.

"This is the *fourth rule:* You have heard what was said of old: 'An eye for an eye, and a tooth for a tooth.' The Pharisees and the scribes teach you to do everything that is written in the old books and what punishment is required for various crimes. There it is said that he who destroys a life must offer up a life for a life, an eye for an eye, a tooth for a tooth, a hand for a hand, an ox for an ox, a slave for a slave, and so on.

"But I say to you: do not fight evil with evil. Not only

should you not demand an ox for an ox, a slave for a slave, or a life for a life, but you should not resist evil. If someone wants to take you to court to sue you for an ox, give him still another; if someone wants to force you to give him your coat, give him your shirt as well; if someone knocks a tooth from one jaw, offer him your other jaw; if you are forced to perform one labor, perform two; if your property is taken from you, give it up; if your money is not returned to you, do not ask for it. And so: judge not, and you will not be judged; punish not, and you will not come before the judgment and will not be punished. Pardon all, and all will be pardoned for you, for if you judge people, they will judge you. Furthermore, you must not judge because we, all people, are blind and do not see the truth. How can I, with eyes full of dust, see the mote in my brother's eye? First I must clean my own eyes, and who among us has clean eyes? If we judge, then we ourselves are already blind. If we judge and punish others, then we are like the blind leading the blind."

Jesus said further: "What, indeed, do we teach? We punish by means of force, with wounds, mutilation, death, that is, with evil—with the very thing forbidden us in the commandment *thou shalt not kill*. That is what we teach others. And what comes of it? We want to teach people, yet we corrupt them. How can it be otherwise that the pupil will learn from and become just like the teacher? What, indeed, will he do when he has learned everything? Exactly what the teacher does: violence, murder.

"And do not think you will find justice in the courts. Leaving the love of justice to human courts is like casting precious pearls before swine: they will trample it and tear it to pieces.

"And so this is the fourth rule: No matter how much you are offended, do not extinguish evil with evil; judge not, and you will not be judged; neither punish nor complain.

"This is the *fifth rule:* The Pharisees and the scribes say: 'Do not bear a grudge in your heart against your brother; expose your neighbor, and you will not suffer for his sin. Kill everyone among your enemies, and take away their wives and cattle; that is, have respect for your countrymen but absolutely no concern for strangers.'

"But I say to you: respect not only your countrymen but strangers as well. Even if strangers have no consideration for you, even if they attack or offend you, honor and oblige them. Only then will you be the true sons of your Father. For him, all are equal. If you are good only to your countrymen, well then, all are good to their countrymen; that is why there are wars. But if you are good to all peoples, then you will be the sons of the Father. All people are his children; therefore, everyone is your brother.

"And so this is the fifth rule: Have the same regard for foreign peoples that I have told you to have among yourselves. There are no enemy peoples, no different kingdoms and kings; all are brothers, all are children of one Father. Do not draw distinctions between peoples according to race or nationality.

"Thus: (1) do not grow angry; (2) do not amuse yourselves with lechery; (3) do not swear anything to anyone; (4) do not judge, and you will not be judged; and (5) do not draw distinctions among various peoples, and know neither kings nor kingdoms.

"And here is yet another teaching for you, which includes all these rules: *All that you wish people to do for you, do unto them.* When you fulfill this teaching, truly, your life will be transformed. You will no longer have any possessions, nor will you need them. Do not set up your life on earth, but build your life in God. Life on earth will perish, but life in God will not perish. Take no thought for your earthly life, for if you think of it, then you will be unable to think of life in God. Where the soul is, there the heart is also.

"And if there is no light in the eyes, then everything is in darkness. And so if you long for and seek darkness, you will fall into darkness. You cannot look to heaven with one eye and to earth with the other; you cannot put your heart into an earthly life and think of God. You will work either for an earthly life or for God. And so beware of any profit. A man's life does not come from what he has but from God. Thus if a man should take possession of the whole world, it would be of no benefit to his soul. And he who would destroy his life to acquire more and more possessions acts foolishly.

"Therefore, have no care over what you will eat and drink or what you will wear. Life is more profound than food and clothing, and God has given you life.

"Behold God's creatures and the birds. They neither sow nor reap nor harvest, yet God feeds them. Surely man is not less than the birds in the eyes of God. If God has given life to man, then he will also manage to feed him. Indeed, you yourselves know that no matter how much care you take, you can do nothing for yourselves. You cannot increase your life-time even by a moment. (The thought is far away, but death is right behind you.)

"And have no care over your clothing. The flowers of the field neither work nor spin, yet they are adorned as even Solomon never adorned himself. If God has so adorned the grass, which grows today but tomorrow will be mowed down, will he not dress you?

"Do not worry and have no care; do not say that we must think of what we are to eat and wear. All people need these things, and God knows of your need.

"Do not worry about what will be; have no anxiety over the future. Live this day. Worry about being in the will of God.

Long only for the one thing that is important, and the rest will come to you of itself. Strive only to be in the will of God, and you will be in it. To him who knocks, it will be opened. To him who asks, it will be given. If you ask for what is of the truth, for what is needful, you will be given what is needful.

"Is there a father who would give his son a stone instead of bread or a serpent instead of fish? How is it, then, that your Father will not give you what you truly need if you ask it of him? And what you truly need is the life of the spirit; ask him for this alone.

"Praying does not mean doing what the hypocrites do in the churches or in front of people. They do this for the sake of people, and from people they receive praise, but not from God. If you wish to enter into the will of the Father, go off so that no one sees you and pray to your Father, who is spirit, and your Father will see what is in your soul and will offer you the true spirit. And do not vainly flap your tongue, as the hypocrites do; your Father knows what you need before you open your mouth.

"And so this is how you must pray: Our Father, let me be in thy kingdom; that is, let thy will be within me. Give me what nourishment I need. And do not call me to judgment for my errors, as I call no one to judgment.

"If you ask the Father for spirit, then call no one to judgment, and the Father will not judge you for your errors. But if you do not forgive people, then God will not forgive you.

"Do nothing for the praise of people. If you act for the benefit of people, then from people will you receive your reward.

"And so if you are compassionate toward people, do not blow your trumpet about it in front of people; that is what the hypocrites do, so that people will praise them. And they get what they want. But if you are compassionate toward others, do good to them in such a way that no one sees you. Your Father will see you and give you what you need.

"And if you suffer need for the sake of God, do not lament and complain to people; that is what the hypocrites do, so that people may see and praise them. All people praise them, and they get what they want. But you must not do this. If you suffer for the sake of God, then walk with a cheerful face, so that people will not see, and your Father will see and will give you what you need.

"Such is the way into the kingdom of God. There is only one way into the will of God; it is straight and narrow. There is always but a single entrance, and all around is a large, broad field; if you walk over it, you will come to the abyss. Narrow is the one path that leads to life, and few walk along it.

"Have courage, though the flock be small. You will enter, for the Father will teach you his will."

Chapter Five

THE FULFILLMENT OF THE LAW

GIVES THE TRUE LIFE

ND JESUS FELT SORRY for the people because they perish without knowing where the true life lies, and because they are tossed about and tormented without knowing why, like sheep abandoned without a shepherd.

And Jesus said to the people: "You are all concerned about the well-being of the flesh; you have harnessed yourselves to a cart you cannot pull and have taken on a yoke that was not made for you. Accept my teaching, follow it, and you will know peace and joy in life. I offer you a different yoke and a different cart—spiritual life. Hitch yourselves to it, and you will learn tranquillity and blessedness from me. You must be of a quiet and gentle heart, and then you will find blessedness in your life. For my teaching is the yoke prepared for you, and the fulfillment of my teaching is an easy cart for you to pull, according to your strength."

And Jesus wandered about the cities and towns and taught everyone the blessedness of life according to the will of God. Then he selected seventy men from his close friends and sent them to those places where he himself wanted to visit.

He said to them: "Many people do not know the blessing of the true life. I feel sorry for them all, and I want to teach them all, but just as the master cannot attend to the harvest of his field, so I do not have time to do this. Go among the various cities and everywhere proclaim the advent of God and the laws of God. Say that for the sake of blessedness one must be a vagrant, that the sum of the law lies in five rules against evil: (1) do not be angry; (2) do not lead a dissolute life; (3) do not take an oath or swear to anything; (4) do not resist evil or pronounce judgments; and (5) do not make distinctions among peoples, and have no regard for kings or kingdoms. Fulfill these rules yourselves, then, in every way.

"First of all, be beggars, vagrants; take with you neither bags nor bread nor money, only the clothes on your back and the shoes on your feet. You are proclaiming the blessedness of beggars, and so you yourselves must be examples of beggary. Choose no hosts wherever you stop off, but stay in the first house you come to. When you arrive at that house, greet the hosts. If they receive you, very well; if not, then go to another house. You will be hated for what you say, and they will attack you and drive you away. And when you are driven out, go to another village, and when you are driven away from there, go to still another. They will drive you away like wolves after sheep, but do not be afraid and do not grow weak, even unto the last hour. And they will take you to court and judge you and flog you and bring you before officials, that you may justify yourselves before them. And when they take you to court, do not be afraid, nor take any thought for what you are to say. The spirit of God will speak from within you what must be spoken. Before you have gone to all the cities, people will understand your teaching and will turn to it.

"Thus, be not afraid. What is hidden in the souls of people will be revealed. What you say to two or three will spread among thousands. The important thing is not to fear those who want to destroy your body. What if they do slay your body? They can do nothing to your soul. And so do not fear them. Fear, rather, the destruction of body and soul if you should stray from the law—that is what you have to fear.

"Five sparrows can be had for a penny, yet even they do not die without the will of God. Nor does a hair fall from a head without the will of God; so what is there to fear, if you are in the will of God? God will be with him who stands before people in the will of God, but God will deny him who denies the will of God before people. Not everyone will believe in my teaching on the need to be beggars and vagrants, on not growing angry or leading a dissolute life, on not swearing and not judging so that you are not judged, on not fighting wars. And those who do not believe will hate it, for it will deprive them of what they like, and there will be strife.

"Like a flame, my teaching will set fire to the world. And so there must be strife in the world. There will be discord in every home. Fathers will be pitted against sons, mothers against daughters, and family members will come to hate those among themselves who accept my teaching. And they will slay them. For one who accepts my teaching, neither father nor mother, wife nor children, nor all his property will have any meaning. Whoever holds father or mother dearer than my teaching has not understood my teaching. Whoever is not prepared at any moment for any torment of the flesh is not my disciple. Whoever is concerned with the life of the flesh will lose his true life, but he who, in keeping with my teaching, destroys the life of the flesh will save his life."

The seventy disciples went out among the cities and towns and did what Jesus commanded. When they returned, they joyfully declared to Jesus: "The diabolical teaching about anger, fornication, oaths, judgment, wars—everywhere it is giving way to us."

And Jesus said to them: "Do not rejoice that evil is giving way to you, but rejoice that you are in the will of God."

And then Jesus rejoiced in the power of the spirit and said: "Because my disciples have understood me and have subdued evil, I see that you are the Highest Spirit, the origin of all things, truly the Father of people. For despite all their knowledge, the wise and the learned could not fathom what the slow-witted have understood by the realization that they are sons of the Father. And you, as the Father, through the love between Father and son, have revealed everything to them. All that man must know is revealed to him through the love of the Father for the son and of the son for the Father. Only he who recognizes himself as a son will be recognized by the Father."

After that, Jesus and his disciples came to a certain house, and so many people crowded around them that they were unable to have their meal.

And members of his household came and wanted to take him away, because they thought he had gone mad.

And the scribes and Pharisees came from Jerusalem and said: "He has gone mad; he wants to correct a lesser evil with a greater evil. He wants to make beggars of everyone, so that there will be no beggars; he wants no one to be punished, so that robbers will kill everyone; he wants no wars, so that our enemies will kill everyone."

And he said: "You say that my teaching is evil, and yet you also say that I destroy evil. This cannot be; evil cannot destroy evil. If I destroy evil, then my teaching cannot be evil, for evil cannot go against itself. If evil were to go against itself, there would be no evil. You yourselves cast out evil according to your law. With what do you cast out evil? With the law of Moses. But this law is from God. I cast out evil with the spirit of God, with the very spirit that has always been within you and is now within you. Only with this can I cast out evil. And the fact that evil is cast out is proof to you that my teaching is true, that the spirit of God is in people and is stronger than carnal lust. If this were not so, then the lust of evil could not be conquered, just as one cannot enter the house of a powerful man and rob him. Thus, people are joined by the spirit of God.

"He who is not with me is against me. He who does not harvest in the field merely scatters the harvest, for he who is not with me is not with the spirit of God and is against the spirit of God.

"And so I say unto you that every human error and every false interpretation will be forgiven, except the false interpretation of the spirit of God. If one utters a word against man, this is nothing, but if one utters a word against what is holy in man—against the spirit of God—then this cannot go unaccounted for. Abuse me as much as you like, but do not deem evil the good that I do. A person cannot be left unaccountable for calling good evil, that is, the deeds that I do. You must either be one with the spirit of God or against it.

"Either consider the tree good and its fruit good or consider the tree bad and its fruit bad, for a tree is valued according to its fruit. You see that I cast out evil; hence, my teaching is good. Anyone who casts out evil, whatever his teaching may be, cannot be against us but is with us, for only the spirit of God can cast out evil."

After this, Jesus came to Jerusalem for the holiday. And at that time, there was a pool in Jerusalem. And of this pool it was said that an angel would step into it, so that the water in the pool would begin to stir, and that after the water was disturbed, whoever first plunged into the pool would be healed of his sickness.

And there were awnings built around the pool. And beneath the awnings lay all the sick, waiting for the disturbance of the water in the pool so that they could plunge into it.

Jesus came to the pool and saw a man lying beneath the awning. Jesus asked him what he was doing there. And the man explained that he had been sick for thirty-eight years and was waiting to be the first into the pool when the water was disturbed, but that he always failed because everyone entered the pool and bathed before him.

Jesus looked at him and said: "It is useless for you to wait here for a miracle from an angel; there are no miracles. There is but one miracle, that God has given life to people, and you must live with all your strength. Do not expect anything here at this pool, but take up your bed and live according to God, as God gives you strength."

The sick man listened to him and got up and walked.

And Jesus said to him: "There, you see what strength you have. See to it that in the future you do not believe all these deceptions; err no more, but live as God has given you the strength."

And the man went and told everyone what had happened to him. And all who had promoted the deception of the pool and profited from it grew angry and did not know how to vent their evil and find fault with the sick man and with Jesus for exposing their deception. They quarreled with the fact that it was the Sabbath and that, according to their law, it was forbidden to work on the Sabbath. First they harassed the sick man, saying: "How dare you take up your bed on the Sabbath? It is forbidden to work on the Sabbath."

The sick man said to them: "The one who raised me up ordered me to take up my bed."

They said: "Who raised you up?"

He said: "I do not know. A man came up and then left."

The Pharisees made their way to Jesus and found him and

said: "How could you order a man to rise and take up his bed on the Sabbath?"

To this Jesus answered: "God my Father will never cease to work, and so I shall never cease to work on weekdays or on the Sabbath. The Sabbath did not make man, but man made the Sabbath."

Then the Jews set upon him even more for having dared to call God his father. And they started to attack him, and Jesus answered them: "Man could do nothing of himself, if God the Father—the spirit of God in man—did not show him what must be done. God, the Father of man, ever lives and acts, and man ever lives and acts. God the Father has given man understanding for the sake of his well-being and has revealed what is good and what is bad.

"Just as God gives life, so the spirit of God gives life. God the Father does not choose, does not decide anything, but having taught man what is good and what is bad, he allows man himself to act. Hence, to honor the spirit of God, people are to obey it within themselves, just as they honor God and obey him. He who does not honor the spirit of God within does not honor God. Understand that he who has given himself over completely to my teaching and has raised up the spirit in himself and has placed his life in it possesses life beyond time and is already delivered from death. It is clear that now the dead will live, having understood the meaning of their lives, that they are the sons of God. For as God lives of himself, so live the sons of God of themselves. The freedom of choice lies in the fact that the spirit of God is in man—this is the whole man.

"Do not be surprised at this teaching; now the time has come for all mortals to be divided. And some—those who do good—will find life, while others—those who do evil—will be destroyed.

"I can choose nothing of myself. I choose what I have

realized from the Father. My choice is just, if I hold not to my desire but to the understanding that I have realized from the Father. If I alone should believe I am right only because I want it so, then you would not believe me. But there is another who assures that I act in truth. It is the spirit of God, and you know that this assurance is true.

"You see from my deeds that the Father has sent me. God the Father has borne and continues to bear witness of me in your souls and in the Scriptures. You have not understood and do not understand his voice, and you have not known and do not know him. His unshakable enlightenment you do not have within you, because you do not believe the one he has sent, the spirit of God in your souls.

"Try to understand your souls. You think to find life in them; you will find the spirit of God within you.

"But you do not want to believe me when I say you will have life.

"It means nothing to me that you pray in your temples and observe the fasts and the Sabbath according to human rules, when the true love for the true God is not within you.

"I teach from my Father and yours, and you do not understand me, while if someone teaches you from himself, you believe him. What can you rely on when you accept the words of one another but do not seek the Son's teaching on the Father? I am not the only one to show you that you are wrong before your Father. Moses himself, in whom you trust, shows you that you are wrong and do not understand him. If you relied on what Moses has said, then you would rely on what I say. If you do not rely on his Scripture, then you will not believe my teaching either."

And in order that they might understand that one may enter into the will of God without effort, he told them a parable.

"A certain king received a kingdom. In order to obtain this

kingdom, the king had to be absent from the kingdom for a time. And so he left.

"But before his departure, he distributed his wealth among his subjects, to each according to his strength: to one went five talents, to another two, to a third one. And he ordered each of them to work while he was gone and to acquire as much as they could with these talents.

"And so the king left, and everyone began to do what he wanted with his master's property. Some went to work, and the one who had five talents earned five more; the one who had one talent earned ten talents; the one who had two talents earned two. Another who had one earned five talents; still another who had one earned one talent. Others still did not work at all with the master's money but took and buried in the earth what they had received from the king and did not work with it. Whoever took five talents was left with five talents. Those who took two and one were left with two and one. And there was yet a third group who did not work for the good of the master, nor did they want to appear before the king, and they sent word to him that they did not want to be under his rule.

"The time came for the king to return to his kingdom, and he summoned all of his subjects to account for what they had done with what had been given to them.

"And a worker came, the one to whom five talents had been given, and he said: 'Look, with five talents I have earned five more.' And another came, the one to whom one talent had been given, and he said: 'Look, from one talent I have earned ten.' The one to whom two talents had been given came and brought two more, and one to whom one had been given brought five more. And still another to whom one was given brought one more.

"And the master equally praised and rewarded them all. To all alike he said: 'I see that you are good and faithful workers.

You have worked for my benefit, and for that I receive you as equal shareholders in my property. We shall rule all together.'

"After this came those subjects who did not work for the good of the master. And one said: 'Lord! You gave me a talent when you left. I know that you are a stern man and want to take from us what you have not given, and I was afraid of you, and out of fear, I hid your talent. Here it is in full. Take back what you have given me.' And others like him who had received five talents and ten talents brought back the master's talents and told him the same thing.

"Then the king said to them: 'Stupid people. You say you hid your talents in the earth out of fear of me and did not work with them. If you knew that I was strict and would take what I did not give, then why did you not do what I commanded? If you had worked with my talents, the property would have increased, and what I had commanded would have been fulfilled, and perhaps I would have mercy on you and it would not be worse for you. But now you still have not escaped my power.'

"And the master took the talents away from those who had not worked with them and ordered the servants to give them to the ones who had earned more.

"And then the servants said: 'Master! They have so much.' But the king said: 'Give to those who have worked for me. For to him who looks after his own, it shall be added, but from him who does not look after his own, the ultimate thing shall be taken away. Cast out these stupid and lazy workers, that they may be no more. And those who sent word that they do not want to be in my power, cast them out, that they may be no more.'

"The king is the origin of life—God the spirit. The world is the kingdom, yet God does not himself govern the kingdom but, like a peasant, has planted the seed and left it alone. On its own, it bears blades of grass, ears of corn and grain. The talent is the enlightenment in every man. God the spirit has placed the enlightenment in people, and he leaves them to live alone according to their will.

"God decides nothing himself, but having imparted all to man, he allows man himself to decide. The talents are not given equally to all, but to each according to his strength. The enlightenment is not given equally to all, but it is given, and for God, there is no more or less. For God, the one thing needful is to work for the enlightenment. Some work with the master's talent; others do not work for the master; still others neither acknowledge nor work for the master. Some people live by the enlightenment; others do not live by it, but it lies dead within them; still others do not acknowledge it. The master has returned and is asking for an account. This is the temporal death and reckoning of life. Some come and say they have worked with the talent; those enter into the life of the master. And the master does not count who has worked more or who less. All are equally given a share in the life of the master. He who will accept the enlightenment will have life.

"He who has the enlightenment and relies on the One who sent it has life beyond time and does not know death but has crossed over into life. Others come and say they have not worked with the talent; they do not refuse the talent but say there is no reason to work, for punishment awaits them whether they work or not. They know the cruelty of the master. Other people have the enlightenment but do not rely on it. They say to themselves: 'Whether you work or not, you will die all the same, and nothing will remain; therefore, there is nothing to be done with it.' To this the king replies: 'If you know I am cruel, then it is all the more needful to do my will. Why did you not try to do it?' If people know that temporal death is unavoidable, then why do they not try to live in the fulfillment of God's will—according to the enlightenment? And the king says: 'Take their talents from them and give to those who have a talent.' It does not matter to the king as to who has the talents, so long as they are there. Just as it does not matter to the peasant which seeds will bring forth ears of corn, so long as there is a harvest. If the enlightenment gives life to people according to their wills, then those who do not hold to it cannot live and stand outside of life. And nothing will remain of them after their temporal death. And to those people who do not acknowledge his power, the king says: 'Cast these out too.' Still other people—those who not only fail to work with the enlightenment and with life but despise the Father of the spirit, who has given it—they cannot live and are also destroyed at death."

Chapter Six

IN ORDER TO RECEIVE THE TRUE LIFE,

MAN MUST RENOUNCE

THE FALSE LIFE OF THE FLESH

OR THE LIFE of the spirit, there can be no distinction between relatives and strangers. Jesus said that his mother and brothers are nothing and mean nothing to him as mother and brothers: the only ones close to him are those who fulfill the will of the God of all.

The blessedness and the life of a person do not rest on his family relationships but on the life of the spirit. Jesus said that those who hold to the enlightenment of the Father are blessed. There is no home for the person who lives by the spirit. Animals have homes, but the person who lives by the spirit can have no home. Jesus said that he has no place designated for him. A designated place is not necessary for the fulfillment of the Father's will, for this is everywhere and always possible. The death of the flesh cannot be terrifying for the man who has given himself over to the will of the Father, for the life of the spirit has nothing to do with the death of the flesh. No anxieties can keep a man from living by the spirit. To the words of the man who said he would fulfill the teachings of Jesus after he had buried his father, Jesus replied: "Only the dead can be concerned about burying the dead, but the living live always in the fulfillment of the will of the Father."

Concerns for family and domestic affairs must not get in the way of spiritual life. He who worries about what the fulfillment of the Father's will might do for his carnal life acts as the plowman who plows looking backward instead of forward. Concerns about the pleasures of carnal life, which seem so important to people, are a dream. The one genuine matter in life is the announcement of the will of the Father, heeding it and fulfilling it. To Martha's reproach that she alone was looking after supper, while her sister Mary was not helping but was listening to the teaching, Jesus replied: "It is wrong of you to reproach her. Look after what concerns you, if you must, but let those who have no need for carnal pleasures do the one thing needful for life." Jesus said: "He who wants to receive the true life that consists of fulfilling the will of the Father must first renounce his personal desires. Not only must he give up arranging his life as he pleases, but he must be prepared for any deprivation and suffering. He who wants to build up his carnal life as he pleases destroys the true life in the fulfillment of the Father's will.

"There is no profit in acquiring anything for the life of the flesh if this acquisition destroys the life of the spirit. More than anything else, self-interest and the acquisition of wealth destroy the life of the spirit. People forget that no matter how much wealth and property they may acquire, they can die at any moment, and their possessions are not needed for their lives. Death hangs over each of us: sickness, murder at the hands of others, accidents—at any second they can cut life short. The death of the flesh is an unavoidable condition of every second of life. If a man lives, he should look upon every hour of his life as a reprieve granted to him out of someone's mercy. This must be remembered, and it must not be said that we do not know it. We know and foresee everything that happens in heaven and earth, yet we forget the death that we know awaits us every second.

"If we are not to forget this, then we cannot give in to the life of the flesh, nor can we rely on it. In order to follow my teaching, you must reckon the profit from serving the carnal life of your own will and the profit from fulfilling the will of the Father. Only he who has made a clear account of this can be my disciple. And he who has made such an account will not regret giving up apparent well-being and apparent life to receive true well-being and true life.

"The true life is given to people, and they know and hear its call, but continually carried away by momentary cares, they deprive themselves of it. The true life is like a feast that a rich man gives and to which he invites guests. He summons the guests just as the voice of the Father's spirit summons all people. But some of the guests are occupied by business affairs, others by their farms, still others by domestic matters, and they do not go to the feast. Only the beggars, who have no concerns of the flesh, go to the feast and are made happy. Just so do people distracted by the cares of carnal life deprive themselves of the true life. He who will not completely renounce all the cares and fears of carnal life cannot fulfill the will of the Father, for one cannot serve oneself a little and the Father a little. You must reckon whether it is profitable to serve your own flesh, whether you can arrange your life any way you please. You must do the same thing a man does when he builds a house or prepares for war. He calculates whether he can finish the building or win a victory. And if he sees that he cannot, then he does not waste his labor or his army. Or else he ruins it all for nothing and will be a laughingstock to people. If you arrange the life of the flesh as you please, then you have to serve the flesh. But since that is impossible, it is better to abandon everything that is of the flesh and serve the spirit, or else there will be neither one nor the other. You will not build up the carnal life, and you will lose the life of the spirit, because in order to fulfill the will of the Father, you must completely renounce the life of the flesh.

"The life of the flesh is that apparent wealth entrusted to us by another, which we are supposed to use to obtain true wealth. If a steward lives with a rich man and knows that no matter how much he serves the master, the master will discharge him and leave him with nothing, then the steward acts wisely if he does good to people while he is in charge of someone else's wealth. Then even if his master abandons him, those to whom he did good will take him in and feed him.

"This is also what people ought to do with their carnal life. Carnal life is the wealth of another, which people control only for a time. If they make good use of this wealth belonging to another, then they will receive their own true wealth. You cannot serve both the false life of the flesh and the spirit; you must serve one or the other. You cannot serve both wealth and God. What seems great in the eyes of people is an abomination before God. In the eyes of God, wealth is evil. The rich man is already guilty for eating much and sumptuously, while beggars go hungry at his door. And everyone knows that the property you fail to give to others is a failure to fulfill the will of the Father."

A wealthy Orthodox official once went up to Jesus and began to boast that he fulfilled all the commandments of the law. Jesus reminded him that there is a commandment to love all people as oneself and that here lies the will of the Father. The official said he also fulfilled this. Then Jesus told him that this was not true: "If you wanted to fulfill the will of the Father, then you would have no possessions. You cannot fulfill the will of the Father if you have possessions that you do not give away to others." And Jesus said to his disciples: "People think they cannot live without possessions, but I say unto you that the true life lies in giving away your possessions to others."

A certain man named Zacchaeus heard the teaching of Jesus and believed in it, and having invited Jesus to his home, he said to him: "I shall give half of my property to the poor and shall give fourfold to anyone whom I have offended."

And Jesus said: "Here is a man who fulfills the will of the Father, for there is no single situation in which the will of God is fulfilled, but our whole life is a fulfillment of it, and this man fulfills it."

The will of the Father of life is that all people return to it.

Good cannot be measured by anything, nor can it be said who has done more and who less. The widow who gives away her last mite gives more than the rich man who gives away thousands. Nor can it be measured by whether or not it is useful. An example of how to do good may be found in the woman who pitied Jesus and senselessly poured over his feet an expensive oil worth three hundred rubles. Judas said that she had acted stupidly, that many could have been fed for this. But Judas was a thief; he lied, and in speaking of the carnal benefit, he was not thinking of the poor. The needful thing is not the benefit, not the amount, but the fulfillment of the will of the Father: to love and live for others.

His brothers and mother once came to Jesus and could not meet with him because so many people were around him. One man saw them, went up to Jesus, and said: "Your family, your mother and brothers, are standing outside; they want to see you."

And Jesus said: "My mother and brothers are those who have fulfilled the will of the Father and go on fulfilling it."

And a certain woman said: "Blessed is the womb that bore you and the breasts you have suckled." To this, Jesus said:

"Blessed always are those who have understood the enlightenment of the Father and keep it."

And a certain man said to Jesus: "I shall follow you wherever you go." And at this, Jesus said to him: "There is no place to follow me, for I have neither home nor any place where I might live. Only the beasts have lairs and dens, but man is spirit, and he is everywhere at home, if he lives by the spirit."

It once happened that Jesus was sailing with his disciples in a boat. He said: "Let us go over to the other side."

A storm rose up on the lake and began to inundate them, so that they nearly drowned. But he was lying on the stern asleep. They woke him and said: "Teacher, does it not matter to you at all that we shall perish?" And when the storm began to grow calm, he said: "How is it that you are so timid? You have no faith in the life of the spirit."

To a certain man, Jesus said: "Follow me." And the man said: "I have an old father who has just died. Allow me first to bury him and then I shall follow you." And Jesus said to him: "Let the dead bury the dead, but you, if you want to live, fulfill the will of the Father and spread it."

Still another man said: "I want to be your disciple and shall fulfill the Father's will, as you command, but allow me first to arrange my household affairs." And Jesus said to him: "If a plowman looks back, he cannot plow. No matter how much you look back, you cannot plow while you are looking behind you. You must forget everything except the furrow you are making; only then can you plow. If you reflect on what will benefit the life of the flesh, then you have not understood the genuine life and cannot live by it."

After this, it once happened that Jesus and his disciples dropped by a certain village. And a woman named Martha invited them to her house.

And Martha had a sister named Mary, who sat at Jesus' feet and listened to his teaching. But Martha was busy seeing that there would be good refreshments. And Martha went up to Jesus and said: "It means nothing to you that my sister has left me alone to serve you. Tell her to work with me."

In answer, Jesus said to her: "Martha, Martha, you worry and busy yourself with many things, but there is only one thing needful. And Mary has chosen the one thing needful, which no one will take from her. Only the nourishment of the spirit is needed for life."

And Jesus said to them all: "Let him who wants to follow me renounce his own will and be prepared for any deprivation and suffering of the flesh at any hour. Only then can he follow me.

"For he who is concerned about his carnal life will destroy the true life. But he who destroys the carnal life, having fulfilled the will of the Father, will save the true life. For what does it profit a man if he gains the whole world but injures or destroys his own life?"

And upon hearing this, a certain man said: "It is well, if there is a life of the spirit, but what if we give away everything and there is no such life?"

To this Jesus said: "You know that the fulfillment of the Father's will gives life to all, but you are diverted from this life by false cares, and you are dissuaded from it. This is what you do: A host prepared a dinner and sent invitations to his guests, but the guests began to decline.

"One said: 'I bought some land, and I have to go look it over.' Another said: 'I bought some oxen, and I have to try them out.' A third said: 'I am getting married and must attend my wedding.'

"And the servants came and told their master that no one was coming. The master then sent his workers to summon the beggars. The beggars did not decline and came. And once they had arrived, there were still seats left.

"And the host sent out more invitations and said: 'Go persuade everyone to come to my dinner so that I shall have more people, but those who declined because they have no time will have no dinner.'

"Everyone knows that the fulfillment of the Father's will gives life, but they do not come, because they are distracted by the deception of wealth."

And Jesus said: "Beware of wealth, for life does not come from having more than others.

"There was once a rich man who had a great harvest of grain. And he thought to himself: 'I shall build storehouses; I shall make them large and gather all my wealth there. And I shall say to my soul: 'Here, soul, everything is in your power; rest, eat, drink, and enjoy your life.'

"And God said to him: 'Stupid man! Your soul will be taken from you this very night, and all that you have hoarded will be left to others.' Thus it happens to anyone who prepares for carnal life and does not live in God."

And Jesus said to them: "You tell how Pilate killed the Galileans. Were these Galileans really so much worse than other people that this should happen to them? Not at all. We are all such people, and we shall all perish if we do not find salvation from death. And those eighteen men upon whom the tower fell when it collapsed, were they really special, worse than all the other residents of Jerusalem? Not at all. If we are not saved from death, then we too shall perish, if not today then tomorrow.

"If we have not yet perished as they have, then we must think thus to ourselves: A man had an apple tree growing in his garden. The master came to the garden to look over the apple tree and saw that there was no fruit on it. The master said to the gardener: 'I have been coming here for three years, and this apple tree is still barren. It must be cut down, for it is taking up space for nothing.' But the gardner said: 'Wait a little while longer, Master. I shall dig around it and put down manure, and we shall see next summer whether it might bear fruit. And if it bears no fruit by next summer, we shall cut it down.'

"Thus are we an apple tree that bears no fruit as long as we live by the flesh and do not bear the fruit of the life of the spirit. It is only by someone's grace that we are left with yet another summer. If we do not bear fruit, we too shall perish, just like the man who built the storehouse, like the Galileans, like the eighteen crushed by the tower, and like anyone bearing no fruit, eternally dying the death.

"No wisdom is needed to understand this; anyone can see it for himself. For not only in domestic affairs but in everything that happens in the world, we know how to judge and guess in advance. If there is a wind from the south, we say it will rain, and so it happens. How is it that we can predict the weather, yet we cannot guess beforehand that we shall all die and perish and that there is only one salvation for us—the life of the spirit, the fulfillment of its will?"

And many people walked with Jesus, and again he said to them all: "Let him who wants to be my disciple have no regard for father, mother, wife, children, brothers, sisters, and all his possessions, and let him be prepared for anything at any hour. And only he who does what I do follows my teaching, and he alone will be saved from death.

"For anyone, before beginning something, will figure out whether it is profitable, and if it is profitable, then he does it; if it is not profitable, then he gives it up. Anyone who is building a house will first sit down and calculate how much money is needed, how much he has, and whether it is enough to finish, so that it will not happen that he does not finish what he started to build and have people laugh at him.

"In the same way, he who wants to live by the life of the flesh must first determine whether he can finish what occupies him.

"And any king who wants to wage war must first consider whether he can go up against thirty thousand men with ten thousand. If he determines that he cannot, then he will send messengers to make peace and will not start a war. Thus, let any man, before giving himself up to the life of the flesh, consider whether he can wage war against death or whether it is stronger than he. And whether it will not be better for him to make peace beforehand.

"Thus, each of you must first examine what you regard as your own: family, money, possessions. And when a man has figured out what benefit there is in this and realizes there is none, only then will he be able to be my disciple.

"The kingdom of heaven does not come in an external form. It cannot be said of the kingdom of heaven, which saves us from death, that it has come or will come, that it is here or there; it is within you, in your soul.

"For if the time comes when you long to find salvation in life and you seek it in some time or other, you will not find it. And if you say to yourself, 'Salvation is here, salvation is there,' do not seek salvation anywhere except within yourself.

"For salvation is instantaneous, like lightning; it is everywhere. There is no time or place for it; it is in your soul.

"As salvation was for Noah and for Lot, so it is and always has been for the Son of man. All life remains the same for all people; everyone eats, drinks, and marries, but some perish, while others are saved.

"There was once an evil judge who feared neither God nor man. And a poor widow went begging to him. The judge would not resolve her case. But the widow begged the judge day and night. The unjust judge said: 'What am I to do? I will resolve the widow's case as she wants; otherwise she will give me no peace.'

"You see that even the unjust judge fulfilled the widow's

request. How, then, can the Father fail to do what is unceasingly prayed of him day and night?

"But besides the Father there is the Son of man, who seeks the truth, and one cannot but believe in him.

"He who will renounce false, temporal wealth for the sake of the true life according to the will of the Father will do what the wise steward does.

"A certain man was once the steward of a wealthy master. And the steward saw that the master was going to turn him out and that he would be left without bread and shelter.

"And the steward thought to himself: 'This is what I shall do: I shall secretly distribute the master's wealth among the peasants and reduce their debts; then, if the master dismisses me, the peasants will remember my good deed and will not abandon me.'

"So did the steward: he summoned the peasants, those who were the master's debtors, and rewrote their bills for them. For those who owed a hundred, he wrote fifty; for those who owed sixty, he wrote twenty, and so on for the others.

"And the master found out about this and said to himself: 'What of it? After all, he has done wisely, for otherwise he would have to go begging. He has caused me a loss, but he has calculated wisely. For in the life of the flesh, we all understand how to calculate truly, but in the life of the spirit, we do not want to understand.'

"We too must deal with the wrong kind of wealth in this way: it must be given away in order to receive the life of the spirit. And if we regret giving up such trifles as wealth for the sake of spiritual life, it will not be given to us. If we do not renounce false wealth, then our own life will not be given to us. One cannot serve two masters at the same time: God and wealth—the will of the Father and one's own will. It is either one or the other."

And the Orthodox heard this, but the Orthodox loved wealth, and so they mocked Jesus.

And he said to them: "You think that because people honor you for your wealth, you are truly honored. No, God does not look at the outside but looks into the heart. And he who is held high before people is vomit before God. The kingdom is now on earth, and great are those who enter into it. Yet the rich do not enter into it, but those who have nothing do. And this has always been so according to your law, according to Moses and the prophets as well.

"Listen to what the rich and the poor are, according to your faith.

"There was once a rich man. He made deals, caroused, and amused himself every day. And there was a vagrant named Lazarus covered with scabs. And Lazarus came to the rich man's courtyard, thinking there might be some scraps left from the rich man's table, but Lazarus did not even get tablescraps. The rich man's dogs ate them all up and even licked the scabs on Lazarus.

"And both of them died, Lazarus and the rich man. And from far away in hell, the rich man saw Abraham in the distance, and with him sat Lazarus, the man with the scabs.

"The rich man said: 'Abraham, Father, with you sits Lazarus, the man with the scabs; he used to wallow at my fence. I dare not trouble you. Let Lazarus, the man with the scabs, come to me; have him dip his finger in water and refresh my throat, for I am burning in fire.' And Abraham said: 'Why should I send Lazarus to you in the fire? In the world, you had everything you wanted, while Lazarus saw only sorrow; thus, it is now for him to rejoice. I could not do it even if I wanted to, because between us lies a great abyss, and it cannot be crossed. We are alive, but you are dead.'

"Then the rich man said: 'Well, then, Father Abraham, let

Lazarus, the man with the scabs, go to my house. I have five brothers, and I pity them; have him tell them everything and show them how harmful wealth is, or else they too will fall into this torment.' But Abraham said: 'They know that it is harmful; Moses and all the prophets have told them so.'

"And the rich man said: 'It would be better if someone resurrected from the dead were to go to them, for they would consider it more carefully.' But Abraham said: 'If they do not listen to Moses and the prophets, they will not listen to one resurrected from the dead.'

"Everyone knows that we must share with our brother and do good to people; the whole law of Moses and all the prophets declares only this. You know it, but you do not want to do it because you love wealth."

And a wealthy Orthodox official went up to Jesus and said: "You are a good teacher. What must I do to receive eternal life?"

Jesus said: "Why do you call me good? Only the Father is good. And if you want to fulfill your life, then fulfill the commandments."

The official said: "There are many commandments; which ones?" Jesus said: "Do not kill, do not fornicate, do not steal, do not lie, honor your father and do his will, and love your neighbor as yourself."

And the Orthodox official said: "I have fulfilled all these commandments since childhood, but I ask you: what more must be done according to your teaching?"

Jesus looked at him and at his rich clothing, smiled, and said: "There is one little thing you have not completed; you have not done as you say. If you want to fulfill these commandments—do not kill, do not fornicate, do not steal, do not lie, and, above all, love your neighbor as yourself—then sell now your whole estate and give it to the poor. Then you will fulfill the will of the Father."

The official heard this, frowned, and went away, because he begrudged giving up his estate.

And Jesus said to his disciples: "Thus you see that there is no way for a rich man to fulfill the will of the Father."

The disciples were terrified at these words. But Jesus repeated it again and said: "Yes, children, he who clings to his own possessions cannot be in the will of the Father. It is much easier for a camel to pass through the eye of a needle than for a rich man to fulfill the will of the Father."

"And they grew more deeply terrified still and said: "If this is so, then a person cannot preserve even his own life."

And he said: "To man it seems that he cannot preserve his own life without possessions, but God preserves the life of man even without possessions."

Jesus was once walking through the city of Jericho. In this city there was an official, a rich tax farmer named Zacchaeus. This Zacchaeus had heard the teaching of Jesus and believed in it. And when he found out that Jesus was in Jericho, he wanted to see him. But there were so many people around him that it was impossible to make one's way through to him.

Then he ran ahead and climbed up a tree so that he could see Jesus when he passed by the tree.

And just as he was walking by, Jesus saw him, and upon finding out that he believed in his teaching, he said: "Climb down from the tree and go home; I shall come to you." Zacchaeus climbed down, ran home, and prepared to meet Jesus and received him with joy.

The people began to judge and to say of Jesus: "Look, he has gone to the house of a tax farmer, a swindler."

In the meantime, Zacchaeus said to Jesus: "This, Lord, is what I shall do: I shall give half of my possessions to the poor, and from the other half I shall pay those whom I have injured."

And Jesus said: "Behold, you are saved. You were dead, and now you live; you were lost, and now you have found yourself. For you have done as Abraham did when he wanted to slay his son in order to prove his faith. For the sum of man's life lies in seeking out and saving what perishes in his soul."

A sacrifice cannot be measured by its size. It once happened that Jesus was sitting with his disciples opposite a poor box. People were placing their money for God into the poor box. And rich men were going up to the poor box and putting a great deal into it. Then an impoverished widow went up and put in two mites.

And Jesus pointed at her and said to his disciples: "You see that this poor widow has put in two mites, yet she has put in most of all; for the others offered what they did not need for their own lives, while this one has offered all she had, has offered her whole life."

Jesus happened to be in the house of Simon the leper. And a woman entered the house. And the woman had a jug filled with precious oil worth three hundred rubles.

Jesus told his disciples that his death was near. The woman heard this and felt sorry for Jesus; she wanted to show him her love and anointed his head with the oil. She forgot about everything, about how much the oil cost, and used up the whole jug anointing his head and feet and poured out all the oil.

And the disciples began to judge among themselves that she had done wrong. And Judas, the one who later betrayed Jesus, said: "Look at how much good has been wasted for nothing. This oil could have been sold for three hundred rubles and could have helped so many beggars." And the disciples started to reproach the woman, and she grew confused and did not know whether she had done good or bad.

Then Jesus said to them: "You trouble this woman for nothing; she has truly done good. And you vainly speak of the beggars. If you want to do good to the poor, then do it; they are always there, so why bring them up? If you feel sorry for the poor, then go, have pity on them, do good to them. But she has had pity on me and has done a genuine good, for she has given away all she had. Who among you can know what is needful and what is not? How do you know that it was unnecessary to pour the oil over me? She has anointed me with oil to prepare my body for burial, and so it is needful. She has truly fulfilled the will of the Father: she forgot about herself and took pity on another, forgot about carnal calculations and gave away all she had."

Chapter Seven

PROOF OF THE TRUTH OF

THE TEACHING

N ORDER TO RECEIVE the true life, one must renounce the life of the flesh. The life of the flesh is food for the true life. The teaching of Jesus consists of renouncing the life of the flesh for the sake of the true life.

The Pharisees and learned men began to ask Jesus: "Very well, you say that the life of the flesh and all its pleasures must be renounced in order to receive the true life, but how do you prove this?"

And Jesus began to groan with pity for these people. Their asking him for proofs showed him that they had not understood him. And he said; "People want proofs, and no proofs can be given to them."

And he said to them: "What carnal proofs do you want for a life that is not carnal? Do you really have no proof of everything you know? Looking at the red evening sunset, you assume that the morning will be fair, and when it is dark in the morning, you assume there will be rain. You have no proofs, but you judge from the appearance of the sky, and you know how to reason. How is it that you do not reason as correctly about your own selves? If you were to consider yourselves as correctly as you do the signs of the weather, then you would know that just as surely as the west wind brings rain, death follows temporal life.

"And so for you there can be no proof of the truth of my teaching other than the teaching itself.

"There can be no proofs of the enlightenment.

"The southern queen came to Solomon not to ask for proofs but to hear his wisdom. The Ninevites did not ask Jonah for proofs but heeded his teaching and were converted; you too must do likewise and not ask for proofs."

After this, the Jews tried to condemn Jesus to death, and Jesus left for Galilee and lived there with his relatives.

The Jewish Feast of the Tabernacles arrived.

And Jesus' brothers planned to go to the feast and summoned Jesus to go with them. They did not believe in the teaching of Jesus and said to him: "Look, you say that the Jewish way of serving God is not right and that you know the genuine way of serving God through deeds. If you really think that no one but you knows the true way of serving God, then come with us to the feast; many people are there. Proclaim before all the people that the teaching of Moses is false. If they all believe you, then it will also be clear to your disciples that you are right. Why hide? You say that our way of serving God is false, that you know the true way to serve God. Well, show it to everyone."

And Jesus said to them: "There is a special time and place for you to serve God, but I have no special time for serving God. I work for God always and everywhere. This is the very thing I show to people; I show them that their way of serving God is false, and for this they hate me. You go to the feast; but I shall go whenever I wish."

And his brothers left, but he remained and arrived later, in the middle of the feast.

And the Jews had been troubled that he did not honor their holiday and had not come. And many argued about his teaching: some said that he spoke the truth, while others said that he only stirred up the people.

In the middle of the feast, Jesus entered the temple and began to teach the people that their way of serving God was false, that God must be served not in the temple or with sacrifices but in spirit and through deeds. They all listened to him and were amazed at his wisdom.

And having heard that they were amazed at his wisdom, Jesus said to them: "My wisdom lies in the fact that I teach what I know from my Father. My teaching consists of fulfilling the will of the spirit, which gives me life. He who does this knows that this is truth. For he will not do what seems good for him but what seems good for the spirit living within him. Your law of Moses is not the eternal law, and so those who follow it do not fulfill the eternal law and do what is evil and false. I teach you the fulfillment of the one will, and in my teaching, there can be no contradiction. But your written law of Moses is filled with contradictions. I give you a teaching by which man becomes higher than all decrees and finds the law within himself."

And many said: "They may say he is a false prophet, but here he condemns the law, and no one says anything to him. Perhaps he is truly genuine; perhaps even the officials recognize him. Only one thing is untrue: it is said that when the one sent from God comes, no one will know where he comes from, but we know his whole family."

All the people failed to understand his teaching, and they all sought external proofs.

Then Jesus said to them: "You know me and where I come from in the flesh, but you do not know where I come from in the spirit. You do not know the One from whom I come in the spirit. It is needful to know him alone. If I were to say that I am the Christ, you would believe me as a man, but you would not believe God, who is in me and in you. One must believe God alone. I am here among you for a brief time of my life; I show you the way of salvation—the return to the source of life from which I arose. But you ask me for proofs and want to condemn me. If you do not know the way, then you surely will not find me when I am no more. You need not judge me but follow me. He who does what I say will find out whether I speak the truth to you. He who does not seek the truth, he for whom the life of the flesh has not become food for the spirit, he who does not seek the truth like water to a thirsty man— that person cannot understand me. But he who thirsts for the truth may go with me and drink. And he who believes in my teaching will receive the true life. He will receive the life of the spirit."

And many believed in his teaching and said: "What he speaks is truth and is from God." Others did not understand him, and they all searched the prophecies for proofs that he had been sent from God. And many argued with him, but no one could refute him.

The Pharisees and the scholars sent their assistants to contend with him. But their assistants returned to them and said: "We can do nothing with him. Never has any man spoken as he does."

Then the Pharisees said: "It means nothing that he cannot be disputed and that the people believe in his teaching. We do not believe, and none of the officials believes; but the people, damn them, are always stupid and unlearned."

And Jesus said to the Pharisees: "There can be no proofs of the truth of my teaching, just as there can be no illumination of the light. My teaching is the true light, the light by which people see what is good and what is bad, and so my teaching cannot be proven; it proves everything else. He who follows me will not be in darkness, but for him, light and life are one and the same."

The Pharisees nonetheless demanded proof of the truth of his teaching and said: "You alone say this."

And he answered them: "Even if I alone say this, it is still the truth, for I know whence I come and where I am going. According to my teaching, life has meaning; according to yours, it has none. Besides, I am not alone in teaching this, but my Father, my spirit, teaches the very same thing. But you do not know him, and this is precisely what proves the falseness of your teaching. You do not know what your life consists of and who the Father of your life is. You do not know whence you come and where you are going. I am leading you, but instead of following me, you discuss who I am, and so you cannot reach the salvation and the life to which I am leading you. And you will perish if you remain in this error and do not follow me."

And the Jews asked: "Who are you?" He said: "I am no one special; as a man, I am nothing. But I am, above all, what I say unto you: I am the way and the truth. I am the enlightenment. And when you make the spirit of the Son of man your God, you will discover what I am, because what I do and say is not from myself as a man but what my Father has taught me—what I speak, I teach.

"Only he who adheres to the enlightenment and fulfills the will of the Father can be taught by me. One must do good to realize the truth. He who does evil loves darkness and moves toward it; he who creates good moves toward the light. And in order to understand my teaching, you must create deeds of goodness.

"He who does good will know the truth, and he who knows the truth will be liberated from evil and from death. For anyone who errs becomes the slave of his error. Just as the slave does not always live in the master's house, but the master's son is always in the house, so does the person who errs in life become the slave of his error—he does not live always but dies. Only he who is in the truth remains forever alive. The truth consists in not being a slave but a son. Thus if you err, you will be slaves, unfree, and you will die. But if you are in the truth, you will be free sons and will live.

"You say of yourselves that you are the sons of Abraham, that you know the truth. Yet you want to kill me for speaking the truth to you. Abraham did not act so. If you want to do this, to kill a man, then you are not sons of God the Father, and you do not serve him but serve your own father. You are not, with me, the sons of the one Father but are the slaves and the sons of error. If, with me, there were one Father for you, then you would love me, because I too issue from God. After all, I was not born from myself but from God. This is precisely why you do not understand my words, and there is no place for my enlightenment within you. If I am from the Father, and you are from the same Father, then you cannot wish to kill me. If you wish to kill me, then we are not from one Father. I am from God, but you are from the devil. You want to do what your father the devil lusts after; he is and always has been a murderer and a liar, and there is no truth in him. If he, the devil, says something, he speaks his own private concern and not what is common to all; he is the father of lie and error, and so you are his sons and the slaves of error.

"You see how easy it is to expose your error. If I err, then expose me; if there is no error, then why do you not believe me?"

And the Jews began to abuse him and said that he was mad. He said: "I am not mad, but I honor my Father, while you want to kill me, a son of the Father; hence you are not my brothers but are the children of another father. It is not I who affirm that I am right, but the truth speaks for me. And so I say to you again: he who comprehends and carries out my teaching will not see death."

And the Jews said: "Well, are we really not speaking the truth, that you are a mad Samaritan? You expose yourself: the prophets died, Abraham died, but you say that he who carries out your teaching will not see death. Abraham died, but you will not die: are you greater than Abraham?"

The Jews all argued about whether or not he, Jesus of Galilee, was an important prophet and forgot everything he told them, that he said nothing about himself as a man but spoke of the spirit of God that was in him.

And Jesus said: "I make nothing of myself. If I were to speak of how things seem to me, everything I said would be meaningless. But there is an origin of all things, which you call God, and he is the one of whom I speak. You have not known and do not know the true God, but I know him. I cannot say that I do not know him. I would be a liar, like you, if I were to say I do not know him. I know him, and I know his will and fulfill it. Abraham, your father, is holy only because he saw and rejoiced in my enlightenment."

The Jews said: "You are thirty years old; how could you have lived in the time of Abraham?"

He said: "Before Abraham was, I was, that 'I' of whom I speak to you: the enlightenment was."

The Jews grabbed stones in order to kill him, but he went away from them.

"I am the light of the world. He who follows me will not walk in darkness, but there will be light in his life. If a man does not see the light, then neither he nor his parents are guilty, but if there is light in him, then his task in life is only to shine for others. As long as we are in the world, we are a light unto the world. If we see people deprived of light, then we reveal to them the light from the source that has produced us. And if a man sees the light, he will be so transformed that no one will recognize him. The man remains the same man. But the difference in him consists of the fact that, having seen he is a son of God, he receives the light and sees what he had not seen before.

"A man who had not seen the light and then sees the light can say nothing as to whether he has truly regained his sight; he can only say: 'I have been reborn, I have become another; I was blind and did not see the true blessing, but now I see. How I came to see, I do not know, but I believe that the one who revealed the light to me is a man from God.'

"And no matter how much a man who has seen the light is told that it is not the genuine light—that he must pray to another God, to the one he does not see; that he who gave him the light is mistaken—that man will not believe it. He will say: 'I know nothing about your God or whether the man who opened my eyes is mistaken; I only know that I saw nothing before, but now I see.'

"And no matter how much such a man is asked how his eyes were opened, he will say only one thing: 'They were opened by my discovery that the origin of life is the spirit, and having discovered this, I was reborn.' No matter how much you declare that the genuine law of God is the law of Moses; that God himself revealed it to Moses; that God associates only with the holy, while the one who opened your eyes is a sinner—the man will answer but one thing: 'I know nothing of this, but I know I did not see, that I was blind, and now I see. And I know that the one who opened my eyes is from God. For if he were not from God, he could not have done this.'

"Such a man relies only on the spirit of the Son of God, who is in him, and needs nothing more."

And Jesus said: "The teaching divides people: the blind are made to see, but those who think they see are struck blind. If people do not see the light from birth, they are not guilty, and they can receive their sight. Only those who assert that they see when they see nothing, only those are guilty."

And the Jews began to argue. Some said: "He is simply mad." Others said: "A madman cannot open people's eyes."

"People give themselves over to my teaching not because I prove it to them; the truth cannot be proven—the truth proves everything else. But people give themselves over to my teaching because it is one and is known to people and promises life. My teaching is for people as the familiar voice of the shepherd is for the sheep when he comes to them through the door to gather and take them to the pasture.

"No one believes your teaching because it is alien to people, and people see your lusts in it. It is to people as it is to sheep that have sight of a man who does not enter by the door but climbs over the fence—the sheep do not know him and take him for a thief.

"My teaching is the one true teaching, like the one door is for the sheep. All your teachings of the law of Moses, all, are a lie, like thieves and robbers to the sheep. He who gives himself over to my teaching will find the true life, just as the sheep will go out and find food if they follow the shepherd. For a thief comes only to steal, rob, and destroy, but the shepherd comes to feed and to give life. And my teaching alone promises the true life.

"The shepherds are masters whose lives are formed by the sheep and who give their lives for the sake of the sheep— these are the true shepherds. But there are mercenaries who do not care about the sheep because they are mercenaries and the sheep are not theirs, so that when a wolf comes, they abandon the sheep; these are not true shepherds. Thus, there are teachers who are not genuine, those who have no concern for the lives of people, and there are the genuine ones, those who give their souls for the lives of people. I am such a teacher.

"My teaching lies in giving my life for the sake of people.

"No one takes my life from me, but I give it freely for the sake of people in order to receive the true life. This commandment I received from my Father. And just as the Father knows me, I know the Father, and so I lay down my life for people. And the Father loves me for fulfilling his commandment. And all people, not only here and now, but all will understand my voice and will come together, and all people will be one, and their teaching will be one."

And the Jews surrounded him and said: "Everything you say is hard to understand and does not agree with our Scripture. Do not torment us but simply tell us outright: are you the Messiah who, according to our books, is to come into the world?"

And Jesus answered them: "I have already told you who I am. I am what I say unto you, but if you do not believe my words, then believe my deeds, the life in God that I lead. By them you will understand who I am and what I have come for. But you do not believe because you do not follow me. He who follows me and does what I say understands me. He who understands my teaching and fulfills it receives the true life. My Father has joined them with me, and no one can divide us.

"I and God the Father are one."

And the Jews were offended by this and took up stones to kill him. But he said to them: "Through my Father, I have shown you much good; why, then, do you want to kill me?"

They said: "We want to kill you not for your good deeds but because you, a man, make yourself into God."

And Jesus answered them: "But this is exactly what is said in your Scripture; it is said that God himself told the bad rulers: 'You are gods.'

"If he deemed depraved people gods, then why do you consider it blasphemy to deem one whom God lovingly sent into the world the Son of God? Every man is in spirit the son of God. If I do not live according to the divine, then do not believe I am the Son of God, but if I live according to the divine, then believe, by my life, that I am in God. And then you will understand that God is in me and I am in Him, that I and the Father are one."

And Jesus said: "My teaching is the awakening of life. He who believes in my teaching, though he may die in the flesh, will live. He who is alive does not die."

And the Jews did not know what to do with him and could not condemn him.

And he went beyond the Jordon and remained there. And many believed in his teaching and said that it was as true as the teaching of John. And so many believed in his teaching.

And Jesus once asked his disciples: "Tell me, how do people understand my teaching about the Son of God and the Son of man?"

They said: "Some understand it to be the same as the teaching of John, others as the prophecy of Elijah. Still others say it is similar to the teaching of Jeremiah. They understand you to be a prophet."

He said: "And how do you understand my teaching?" And Simon Peter said to him: "In my view, your teaching consists in your being the chosen son of the God of life. You teach that God is the life in man."

And Jesus said to him: "Happy are you, Simon, that you have understood this. Man could not have revealed this to you, but you have understood it because the God in you has revealed it to you. Neither carnal reasoning nor I with my words has revealed this to you, but God, my Father, has revealed it directly to you.

"And the gathering of people for whom there is no death is based on this enlightenment."

Chapter Eight

THERE IS NO OTHER LIFE

OU WILL BE BEGGARS, vagrants; you will be humbled. But he who loves father or mother, son or daughter, more than he loves me has not understood my teaching. He who is not prepared for all suffering of the flesh has not understood me. He who acquires nicer and nicer things for the life of the flesh will destroy the true life. But he who destroys his carnal life will receive the true life."

At these words, Peter said to him: "All this is true, and we have served you and have cast aside all cares, all property; we have become vagrants and have followed you. What will be our reward for this?"

Jesus said to him: "You yourself know what you have given up. And anyone who forsakes family, sisters, brothers, father, mother, wife, children, and property and follows my teaching of the true blessedness—shall he not receive a hundred times more even now, in this life, of sisters, brothers, and fields and all he needs? And in addition to everything in this life, he receives life beyond time. As for your thought that you will receive a reward for what you have done, you are mistaken.

95

There are no rewards in the kingdom of God. The kingdom of God is itself the good and the reward. In the kingdom of God all are equal; there are neither those who are first nor those who are last.

"This is what the kingdom of God is like: A certain master went out one morning to hire workers for his orchard. He hired the workers for a penny a day, took them to the orchard, and put them to work.

"Again, at noon, he went out to hire still more and sent them to work in the orchard. And he agreed on a penny a day with all of them.

"It came time to pay them, and the master ordered that they all be paid the same amount, first those who came last and then those who came first.

"The ones who came first saw that those who came last were given a penny. And they thought they would be given more. Then those who came first were also given a penny. They took it and said: 'What is this? They have worked only one section, while we have all done four; why are we given the same amount? This is unfair.'

"But the master walked up and said: 'Why are you grumbling? Have I treated you badly? I have given you what I hired you for. We agreed on a penny. Take what is yours and go. If I want to give the last what I have given you, is it not in my power to do so? Or is it because you see I am good that you have become so envious?'

"In the kingdom of God, there are neither those who are first nor those who are last; all are one. He who fulfills the will of God and renounces the life of the flesh has the life of the spirit. And those who fulfill it are in the will of God. And no other person can draw a man to the will of God. The kingdom of God is won by one's own effort."

Two of his disciples, James and John, once went up to Jesus and said: "Teacher, promise us that you will do for us what we ask of you."

He said: "What do you want?" They said: "To be as you are."

And Jesus said to them: "You ask what is not in my power. You can live as I do and be reborn through the spirit, as I am, but it is not in my power to make you into what I am. All people are born differently, and each is given a different level of enlightenment, but everyone alike can fulfill the will of God and receive life."

Having heard this, the other disciples grew angry at the two brothers for wanting to be like the teacher and to be the most superior of the disciples.

Jesus summoned them and said: "If you brothers, James and John, asked me to make you into what I am in order to be the most superior disciples, then you made a mistake. And if you other disciples are angry at them because these two want to be more advanced than you, then you have also made a mistake. Only in the world do kings and officials matter, those who are more advanced for ruling the people. But among you, there can be no one who is superior or inferior. Among you, in order for one to be greater than the other, he must be a servant to all; for in the teaching of the Son of man, he does not live to be served but to serve all to renounce his carnal life as a redemption for the life of the spirit. God the spirit seeks salvation for him who perishes. God longs for the salvation of people and rejoices in it, as the shepherd does when he finds a lost sheep. And when one is lost, he leaves the ninety-nine and goes to save the lost one. And if an old woman loses a kopek, she will sweep out the whole cottage and search until she finds it. God loves him who perishes and calls him unto himself."

And he told them another parable showing that one who lives in the divine will must not be exalted. He said: "If you are summoned to a dinner, do not sit down in the place of honor, lest someone more esteemed than you should come and the host say: 'Go away and let the one who is better than you sit down.' Then you would be shamed even more. It is better for you to sit in the most humble place; then the host will find you and call you to an honored place, and you will be honored.

"Thus, in the kingdom of God, there is no room for pride. He who exalts himself thereby lowers himself, but he who is humble (considering himself unworthy) thereby raises himself in the kingdom of God.

"A certain man had two sons. The younger one said: 'Father, give me my due share.' And the father gave it to him.

"The younger one took his portion and went to a foreign land; he squandered his possessions and came to live in poverty. He ended up as a swineherd in that foreign land. And he was so hungry that he ate acorns with the swine. One day he reflected on his life and said to himself: 'Why did I divorce myself from my father? My father has much of everything. A hundred workers eat at my father's house, while I am eating the same food as the swine. I know: I shall go to my father, fall down at his feet, and say, "I am guilty before you, Father. I am not worthy to be your son; just take me in as a farmhand."'

"So he thought and went to his father. And when he was walking up, his father immediately recognized him in the distance and himself ran out to meet him and embraced him and began to kiss him.

"And the son said: 'Father, I am guilty before you; I am not worthy to be your son.' But his father did not listen and said to the workers: 'Bring at once the very best clothes and the finest shoes and put them on him. And run and catch a fatted calf and kill it. We shall celebrate, for this is my son who was dead but has now come back to life. He was lost, and now he is found.'

"The older brother came from the field, and as he approached the house, he heard them singing inside. He called a boy over to him and said: 'What is this merriment in our house?' And the boy said: 'Haven't you heard? Your brother has returned, and your father is rejoicing; he ordered the fatted calf to be killed to celebrate his son's return.'

"The older brother was greatly offended and did not go into the house. But when the father came out to him and called him, he said: 'Father, I have worked for you for so many years, and I do not disobey your command, yet you have never slaughtered a fatted calf for me. But my younger brother left home and squandered his property with drunkards, and for him, you have slaughtered a fatted calf.' The father said: 'You have always been with me, and everything that is mine is yours. But how can I fail to rejoice that your brother was among the dead and has returned to life, that he was lost and is found?'

"In the same way, your Father in heaven does not want a single person, even the most unworthy, to be lost but to live.

"The lives of people who do not understand that they live in this world not to eat, drink, and make merry but to work their whole lives for God—the lives of these people are like this: A master planted an orchard; he worked it, cultivated it, and did everything so that the orchard would yield as much fruit as possible. And he sent workers into the orchard, so that they worked and gathered the fruit and paid him for the orchard according to their agreement.

"The master is God. The orchard is the world. The workers are people. God created the world and sent people into it only so that people might return to God what is divine, the enlightenment of life that he has placed within them. The time has come; the master has sent the workers for the rent. God is in the souls of people, constantly speaking to them of what they must do for Him, constantly summoning them.

"The workers drove away the master's messenger with nothing and continued to live imagining that the orchard is their own and that they themselves occupy it by their own grace. People drove away the one who reminded them of God's will and continued to live imagining that they live for themselves, for the pleasures of carnal life.

"Then the master sent more and more of his beloved ones, sent his own son, to remind the workers of their debt. But the workers went completely crazy and imagined that if they killed the master's son who reminded them that the orchard was not theirs, then they would be left in peace. And they killed him. People do not like reminders of the spirit that lives within them and shows them it is eternal, while they are not eternal. And they have killed the consciousness of the spirit as much as they could; they have wrapped the talent given to them in a handkerchief and buried it.

"What is the master to do? Only this, to drive out those workers and send others. What is God to do? To sow as long as there might be fruit. And this is what he does. People have not understood and do not understand that the consciousness of the spirit within them, which they conceal because it disturbs them, is the enlightenment itself and is the sole basis of life. They reject the stone by which everything is supported. And those who do not choose the life of the spirit as their foundation do not enter the kingdom of God and do not receive life. In order to receive life and the kingdom of God, you must be mindful of your situation; you must expect no reward and feel yourself in debt."

Then the disciples said to Jesus: "Increase faith within us. Tell us something, that we may believe more firmly in the life of the spirit and not regret the life of the flesh. So much must be renounced, all must be renounced, for the life of the spirit. But as you yourself have said, there is no reward."

And at this, Jesus said to them: "If you had faith such as the faith that a large tree will grow from a birch seed, then you would believe that within you is the embryo of the life of the spirit, from which the true life grows. Faith does not consist of a belief in some amazing thing; faith consists of understanding your condition and realizing where salvation lies. If you understand your condition, you will not expect a reward, but you will labor to preserve what has been given to you. If you come from the field with a worker, you will not seat him at the table but will order him to put away the livestock and prepare your supper, and then you will say to him: 'Eat and drink.' You do not thank the worker for doing what he ought to do. Nor is the worker offended, but he works and expects what he ought to expect.

"Just so should you do what you ought and take yourselves for worthless workers who have done only what they are supposed to do and expect no reward. The concern is not to receive a reward but to avoid being a guilty, bad worker. We must not be concerned with the belief that there will be a reward and life—this cannot be otherwise; rather, we must be concerned that we do not destroy this life and do not forget that it is given to us to bring forth its fruits and fulfill the will of God, without thinking of what we have fulfilled and what is our due reward.

"Only then will you realize that the kingdom of God of which I speak to you exists, that this divine kingdom is the one salvation from death, and that it will not appear in such a way that it can be seen. With regard to the kingdom of God that saves us from death, it cannot be said that it has come or it will come, that it is here or it is there. It is within you, in your soul. Thus, if the time comes when you long to find salvation in life and if you should seek it in some time or other, you will not find it. And if you are told that salvation is here, salvation is there, do not seek salvation anywhere except within your own self. For salvation, like lightning, is instantaneous, and for it, there is no time, no death; it is within you.

"And as salvation was for Noah, as it was for Lot, so it is

always for the Son of man. Life remains the same for all people; everyone eats, drinks, and marries, but when the deluge comes and the rain from heaven, when the death of the flesh comes, some will perish, while others will be saved. When, for you, the kingdom of God is established within you, then none of you will think of the flesh any longer, and you will not look back, as Lot's wife did. You cannot plow if you are looking backward. Be mindful only of the present."

The disciples still asked how to find out that this has taken place, that the day of salvation has come and that they have attained eternal life.

And Jesus answered them: "No one can know when and where it will happen to a man. It cannot be shown or proven. One thing you can know is that when it is completed within you, you will feel the true life within yourself. What will happen to you is what happens to a tree in the spring: it was dead, and now you see the branches begin to soften, the buds fill out, and the leaves grow. This is what you will feel within yourself. You will feel life within you and life issuing from you. When you feel this, then know that the kingdom of God and the day of salvation are near. Therefore do not be concerned about the life of the flesh. Seek only to be in the will of God, and everything else will come of itself."

And he told them they must wish for this alone and not to lose heart.

And the disciples said to him: "Teach us to pray."

And he said: "Your whole prayer should be only this: Father! Let your spirit be holy within us, and may your will be within us. Let us feed on the life of the flesh for the sake of the life of the spirit. Do not be strict in exacting from us what we owe you, that we may not exact from others who owe us; do not call us to reckoning.

"After all, if a son asks his father for bread, the father will not give him a stone, nor will he give him a serpent instead of a fish. If we, evil men, give to our children what is good for them and not what is evil, then how can our Father, from whom we have arisen, the Father of the spirit, fail to give us the spirit that is the one thing we ask of him? Not only no father but no stranger can deny another if he is persistently beseeched. If you go to your neighbor even at midnight to ask for bread to treat your guest, you know that, if not from friendship then from conscience, he will give you what you need if you beseech him. Ask, and you will receive; knock, and it will be opened. You must not expect God to give to you of the spirit that saves from death, if you neither seek nor ask him."

And Jesus said: "There was an evil judge who feared neither God nor man. And a poor widow petitioned him. The judge would not resolve her case. But the widow clung to the judge and beseeched him day and night. And the judge said: 'What am I to do? I shall decide the widow's case as she desires, else she will give me no peace.'

"You understand that even an unrighteous judge did this. How, then, can God fail to do what is constantly prayed of him day and night? If there is a God, then he will do it. If there is no God but, instead, an unrighteous judge, there is nonetheless the Son of man, who seeks the truth, and one cannot help but believe in him. Seek always the kingdom of God and its truth, at every moment, and the rest will come of itself. Do not be concerned about the future, but strive only to avoid the evil of the present.

"Be forever prepared, like servants awaiting the master to open the door immediately for him when he comes. The servants do not know when he will return, early or late, and must always be prepared. And if they greet the master, then they have fulfilled his will, and it is pleasing to him. Just so is it in life; always, always, at every minute of the present, one must live through the life of the spirit, taking no thought for past or future, without saying to oneself: 'At that time, I shall do such and such.' If the master knew when the thief would come, he would not sleep; thus, you must never sleep, because, for the life of the Son of man, there is no time. He lives only in the present and does not know when his life begins and ends. Our lives are like the life of a slave whom the master has left as a watchman in his home. Happy is the slave who always does the will of his master. But if he says, 'The master will not come soon,' and forgets about the master's affairs, then the master will return unawares and drive him out. And so do not lose heart, but live always in the present through the spirit. For life, there is no time.

"Look after yourselves, so that you do not aggravate yourselves and obscure yourselves with drunkenness, gluttony, and worries and let the time of salvation slip by. The time of salvation is cast over everyone like a net; it is always now. And so live always through the life of the Son of man.

"The kingdom of heaven is like this: Ten maidens went out with their lamps to meet the bridegroom. Five were wise, and five were foolish. The foolish ones took the lamps but brought no oil. The wise ones took the lamps and a supply of oil. While they were waiting for the bridegroom, they dozed off.

"When the bridegroom approached, the foolish ones saw that they had little oil. They started to ask for some and then went to buy it. But while they were gone, the bridegroom entered, and the wise maidens, who had oil, entered with him, and the doors were closed. All the maidens had to do was meet the bridegroom with their lamps, yet they had forgotten that the needful thing was not that the lamps burn but that they burn at the proper time. But in order for them to burn at the proper time, they must burn constantly. The purpose of life is only to exalt the Son of man, and the Son of man is always present; he is not in time. Therefore he must be served beyond time, in the one present. And so make an effort, do the deeds to enter into the life of the spirit; if you do not make an effort, you will not enter.

"You will say: 'We have stated such and such.' But there will be no good deeds, and there will be no whole life. For by his power, the Son of man will give to each what he has accomplished.

"People are all divided according to how they serve the Son of man. And by their deeds, they are divided into two groups, like a flock of sheep separated from the goats. Some will live; others will perish. Those who have served the Son of man will receive what has belonged to them from the beginning of the world, the life that they have preserved. And they have preserved that life by serving the Son of man: they have fed the hungry, clothed the naked, taken in the stranger, visited the prisoner. They have lived through the Son of man; they have felt that he is one in all people, and so they have loved him. He is one in all. Those who have not lived through the Son of man, who have not served him, have not realized that he is one in all, and so they have not joined with him. They have lost the life in him and have perished."

Chapter Nine

TEMPTATIONS: MAN LIVES BY THE
LIFE OF THE SPIRIT IN THE FLESH

F A MAN lives for the flesh, then he perishes, like all flesh. If he lives by the spirit, then he obtains the true life, but the flesh tempts him. Beware of temptations. For it is better that one of your limbs perish than your whole body. Better to forfeit a minute of enjoyment than to lose the true life. The true life is given to us, and we all know it, but the deception of the flesh ensnares us.

Children were once brought to Jesus, that they might be with him for a while. But the disciples started to drive away the children, saying: "What does our teacher have to do with stupid kids?"

Jesus saw that they had no respect for the children and were chasing them away. He became distressed with the disciples and said: "You have no reason to drive away the children like this; they are the very best of people, because all children live in the will of God. Truly, they are already in the kingdom of God. You must not chase them away but learn from them, for in order to live in the will of God, you must live as children live. Children always fulfill the *five rules* I have given you: children do not curse, do not bear evil toward people; children do not fornicate; children do not swear to anything; children do not resist evil, nor do they judge anyone; children do not know the difference between their own people and a foreign people and do not wage war. Children fulfill the five rules, and so they are better than adults, and they are in the kingdom of God.

"If you do not cast aside all the deceptions of the flesh and become as children, you will not enter the kingdom of God.

"Only he who realizes that children are better than we are because they do not violate the law of God—only he understands my teaching. And only he who understands my teaching understands God.

"We must not despise children, for they are better than we, and their souls are pure before God and are always with God. They are all good and kind. Not one child perishes by the will of God, but they are all destroyed only by people, for people falsely lure them away from the good.

"And so we must care for them and not falsely lure them away from the Father and from the true life. The man who falsely lures them away from purity does evil. To entice a child away from good—to tempt him with anger, fornication, swearing, judgment, and war—is just as bad as hanging a millstone around the child's neck and throwing him into the water: it would be hard for him to swim out, and he would drown. Likewise, it is hard for a child to refuse a temptation into which an adult leads him.

"It is only because of temptations that the world of people is unhappy. Temptations are everywhere in the world; they always have been and always will be, and man perishes from temptations.

"So give up everything, sacrifice all, if only to keep from falling into temptation. When a fox falls into a trap, he will twist off his paw and run away, and he will stay alive. You should do the same; give up everything, if only to keep from becoming entangled in temptations. Temptations are pitted against all five rules, and you must beware of all of them.

"Beware, then! This is the temptation against the first rule, *be not angry.*

"Do not ask how many times you must forgive your brother; do not think you may forgive seven times and then take revenge. Forgive not seven times but seventy times seven, and then forgive again.

"For the kingdom of God may be likened unto this: A king set out to settle accounts with his tax debtors. And a debtor who owed him a million rubles was brought to him. And he had nothing to give. The king would have had to sell the man's estate, wife, children, even the debtor himself. But the debtor began to beg for mercy from the king. And the king took mercy on him and forgave him the entire debt.

"Then the debtor set off for home and saw a peasant along the way; the peasant owed him fifty kopeks. The man who owed the king grabbed him and started to strangle him and said: 'Give me what you owe me!' And the peasant fell to his feet and said: 'Have patience with me; I'll give you back everything.' But the debtor showed no mercy and had the peasant put into prison, where he would stay until he paid back everything.

"The other peasants saw this and went to the king and told him what the tax debtor had done. Then the king summoned the debtor and said to him: 'You evil dog, I forgave you all your taxes because you implored me. And you should have shown mercy to your debtor, just as I showed mercy to you.' And the king became angry and turned over the debtor to be tortured until he paid the whole tax.

"Just so will God the Father do to you if you do not forgive with all your heart everyone who is guilty before you.

"If a man offends you, remember that he is a son of the one God, of the Father, and is your brother. If he offends you, go and appeal to his conscience face to face. If he listens to you, then you will profit by having a new brother.

"If he does not listen to you, then appeal to his conscience and call two or three men to go with you to persuade him. If he does not listen to them, then tell the assembly, and if he does not listen to the assembly, then he will be a stranger to you. Forgive him and have nothing to do with him.

"You know, after all, that if an argument arises with a man, it is better to reconcile with him without going to court. You know and you act accordingly, because you know that you have more to lose if you go to court. Well, it is the same with any argument; if you know that it is bad and will lead you to create a distance between you and God, then divorce yourself from evil immediately and make peace, before the one with whom the evil began goes away.

"After all, you yourselves know that as it is bound on earth, so it will be before God, and what you unleash on earth is unleashed before God.

"Again, you must realize that if two or three agree in everything on earth, then they will receive from the Father all they ask for. For where two or three are united through my teaching, they fulfill my teaching.

"Beware! This is the temptation against the second rule, *do not fornicate.*"

Some false preachers once went up to Jesus and, testing him, said: "Is a man allowed to abandon his wife?" He said: "In the beginning, man was created male and female; this is natural law.

"And because of this, a man leaves his father and mother and clings to his wife, and husband and wife merge into one. Thus, man must not violate natural and divine law and divide what has been joined together. And if it happens, according to your Mosaic law, that a man may cast aside his wife, then this is false; according to natural law, it cannot be.

"I say unto you that whoever casts aside his wife drives into debauchery both her and the one who takes up with her."

And the disciples said to Jesus: "If one must be bound to the same wife once he has taken her and never abandon her, that is so difficult that it is better not to marry at all."

He said to them: "One need not marry, but you must understand what this means. If a man wants to live without a wife, then he is to be completely pure and not touch a woman. There are men who do not like women at all, but whoever loves women is to be joined with one woman and neither cast her aside nor long for other women.

"Beware! This is the temptation against the third rule, *do not promise anything to anyone.*

"Your false preachers travel around everywhere and lead the people to swear oaths that they will be loyal to the law and to the authorities, but in this they only lead people astray. It is impossible to promise your body for your soul, for in your soul is God, and people cannot make promises for God before people."

And a tax collector once went up to Peter and asked him: "Well, then, does your teacher not pay taxes?"

Peter said: "No, he does not pay taxes." And he went and told Jesus that he had been stopped and was informed that they were all obligated to pay taxes. Then Jesus said to him: "A king does not collect taxes from his sons, and other than the king, they are not obligated to pay anyone, right?

"So it is with us. If we are sons of God, then we are not obligated for anything to anyone except God; we are free before everyone. We are not obligated for anything, but if taxes are demanded of you, then offer them, not because you are bound but because you must not resist evil. And if they demand of you your coat, offer them also your shirt."

Another time, the preachers got together with the king's officials and went to Jesus to trap him with words.

They said to him: "You teach according to the truth, so tell us, are we obligated to pay taxes to Caesar or not?"

Jesus realized that they wanted to condemn him for opposition to the oath to Caesar. He said to them: "Show me what you use to pay taxes to Caesar." They gave him a coin. He looked at the coin and said: "What is this here? Whose image and signature?"

They said: "Caesar's."

And he said: "Then offer to Caesar what is Caesar's, but your soul, which is God's, offer to no one except God. Money, property, your labor—give it all to anyone who asks it of you, but offer your soul to no one except God. And make no promises to anyone, because you are all in the power of God; offer your soul to God alone.

"Beware, then! This is the temptation against the fourth rule, *judge not and you will not be judged.*"

Jesus' disciples once stopped off at a village and asked to spend the night. They were not allowed. Then the disciples went to Jesus and complained about this and said: "May they be struck by lightning for this."

Jesus said: "None of you understands what you are in spirit. I do not teach how to destroy but how to save."

A woman was once brought to Jesus, and the people told him: "This woman has been caught in adultery. According to the law, she should be stoned to death. What will you say?"

Jesus answered nothing but waited for them to change their minds. But they pressed him and asked how he would judge the woman. Then he said: "Let him among you who is without error cast the first stone at her." Then the Pharisees looked at each other, and their conscience reproached them; those who were in front went to hide behind those who were in the rear, and then they all went away.

And Jesus was left alone with the woman. He looked around and saw no one. "Well," he said, "does no one accuse you?" She said: "No one." And he said: "Then I cannot accuse you. Go, and err no more."

No matter how evident, no matter how bad the deed might be, no one is to be accused of it. Only he in whom there is no error could accuse, yet to accuse is itself already an error.

A man once came to Jesus and said: "Order my brother to give me my inheritance."

Jesus said to him: "No one has made me a judge over you, and I judge no one. Nor can you judge anyone.

"Beware, then! This is the temptation against the fifth rule, *there are no different peoples*. All people are brothers, sons of one God the Father."

A certain lawyer wanted to tempt Jesus and said: "What must I do to receive the true life?"

Jesus said: "You know: love God your Father and love your brother, whether he is a fellow countryman or not." And the lawyer said: "That would be fine if there were not various peoples, but how am I to love the enemies of my people?"

And Jesus said: "There was once a Jew who fell into misfortune. He was beaten, robbed, and thrown out onto the road. A Jewish priest came along, looked at the beaten man, and walked on by. A Levite came along, looked at the beaten man, and walked on by. Then a man from a foreign, hostile people came along, a Samaritan. This Samaritan saw the Jew and took no thought for the fact that Jews have no regard for Samaritans; he took pity on the beaten Jew. He washed him off, dressed his wounds, and took him on his ass to an inn. He paid the innkeeper money for the beaten man and promised to drop in later and pay more. That is how you are to treat foreign peoples, those who have no consideration for you and bring you to ruin; then you will receive the true life."

Jesus said: "The world of temptations loves its own and

hates what is of God; and so the people of the world—priests and biblical scholars—will torment those who fulfill the law of God. I too am going to Jerusalem, and I shall be tormented and killed, but my spirit cannot be killed; it shall live."

Hearing that Jesus would be tortured and killed in Jerusalem, Peter became distressed, took Jesus by the hand, and said to him: "If this is so, then it is better not to go to Jerusalem." Then Jesus said to Peter: "Do not say that. What you say is a temptation. If you fear torture and death for me, it means you are thinking of the human and not of the divine.

"Nothing evil can happen to him who lives by the light of the enlightenment, because he is ever in the light. Evil can befall only him who moves out of the light of truth and into the darkness of carnal temptation."

After summoning the people along with his disciples, Jesus said: "Let him who wants to live according to my teaching renounce his carnal life; let him be prepared for all sufferings of the flesh, for he who fears for the life of the flesh destroys the true life. But he who scorns the life of the flesh saves the true life."

And he told them that if a person who lives by the enlightenment is killed, the enlightenment will not die but will live.

And they did not understand this. And the Sadducees came up to him, and he explained everything that the true life in God and rising from the dead mean. The Sadducees said that after the death of the flesh there is no life of any kind. They said: "How can everyone be resurrected from the dead? If everyone were resurrected, there is no way all those resurrected could live together.

"We had seven brothers, you see. The first one married and died. His wife went to the second brother, and he died; then she went to the third and so on up to the seventh. How, then, are these seven brothers to live with one wife if they are all resurrected?"

Jesus said to them: "You purposely confuse things and do not understand the nature of God and life after death. People in this life marry, but those who earn life after the death of the flesh do not marry because there is no need for them to continue life in others; they themselves never die because they are united with God, having been made into his sons.

"It is written in your Scriptures that God said: 'I am the God of Abraham, of Jacob.' And God said this when, for people, Abraham and Jacob were already dead. Hence, those who have died for people are alive for God. If there is a God and God does not die, then those who are with God are always alive. Restoration from death is life in God. Life in God is the fulfillment of the will of God in carnal life. He who fulfills the will of God is united with God. For God, there is no time, and so, being united with God, man departs from time and therefore from death."

Upon hearing this, the preachers did not know what to devise in order to silence him; they joined with lay people and together they began to interrogate Jesus.

And one of them, a preacher, said: "Teacher! Which, in your opinion, is the highest commandment in all the law?" The preachers thought Jesus would grow confused in answering something on the law. But Jesus said: "The highest commandment is to love the Lord God, in whose power we are, with all our soul. And another follows from it: to love your neighbor, since the Lord is in him. In these two commandments lies everything written in all your books."

And Jesus said further: "Who, in your view, is the Christ? Is he anyone's son?" They said that in their opinion Christ is the son of David. Then he said to them: "How, then, is David to call Christ his lord? Christ is not the son of David, is not anyone's son; rather, Christ is the very lord, our master, whom we know within ourselves as our life. Christ is the enlightenment that is in us." They asked him nothing more after this.

And Jesus said: "Look and beware of the leaven of the false preachers. Beware of the leaven of the worldly and the leaven of the kingly. But above all, beware of the leaven of the false preachers, for this is deception."

And when the people understood what he was talking about, he said: "Above all, beware of the teaching of the learned false preachers. Beware of them, for they have supplanted the prophet who announced to the people the will of God. Out of self-interest, they have taken over the power to preach to the people the will of God. They preach words but do nothing. Thus, they say to do this or that but do nothing, because they do nothing good but only talk. They speak of what must not be done and themselves do nothing. They struggle only to retain their right to teach, and for this, they try to distinguish themselves: they array themselves in fine clothes and honor themselves with rituals. Know, then, that no one is to call himself teacher or preacher. Our Lord alone is teacher, is preacher. But the preachers call themselves teachers and by this prevent us from entering the kingdom of God and themselves do not enter.

"These preachers think one may be led to God by external ceremonies and oaths. Like blind men, they do not see that externals mean nothing, that everything lies in a person's soul. They do the easiest of outward things, but what is needful and difficult—love, kindness, truth—they forsake. They care only about being within the law outwardly and outwardly leading others to the law. And so they are like painted tombs that appear to be clean on the outside but are an abomination on the inside. Outwardly they honor the holy martyrs, when in fact they are the very ones who torment and kill holy men.

"From the first and even now, they are the enemies of everything good. All the evil in the world comes from them, because they conceal the good and set forth evil in its place. False preachers must be feared above all.

"For you yourselves know that any error may be corrected. But if people mistake what is good, this error cannot be corrected. And this is precisely what the false preachers do."

And Jesus said: "Here in Jerusalem, I wanted to unite all people into the one enlightenment of the true blessedness, but the people here know only how to put to death the teachers of the good. And so they remain the same godless people they were before; they will not know God as long as they do not accept in love the enlightenment of God."

And Jesus went away from the temple. Then his disciples said to him: "What about this temple of God with all the adornments that people have brought to it for the sake of God?"

And Jesus said: "Verily I say unto you, this whole temple, with all its adornments, will be destroyed, and nothing will remain of it.

"There is but one temple of God: the hearts of people when they love one another." And they asked him: "When will there be such a temple?" And Jesus said to them: "It will not be soon. Many more people will create deception through my teaching, and because of this, there will be wars and insurrections. And there will be much lawlessness and little love. But when the true teaching is spread among all people, there will be an end to evil and temptations."

Chapter Ten

THE STRUGGLE WITH TEMPTATIONS

FTER THIS, the preachers and archpriests sought with all their power to trap Jesus in order somehow to destroy him. They gathered in a council and began to pronounce judgments. They said: "We must somehow put an end to this man. He demonstrates his teaching in such a way that if we leave him alone, everyone will believe in him and cast aside our faith. Even now, half the people already believe in him. And if they believe in his teaching that man is the son of God, that no one is obligated to obey, that all people are brothers, that nothing special distinguishes our Jewish people from other peoples—then the Romans will take us over completely and destroy all our laws and our whole faith, and there will no longer be a Jewish kingdom."

The preachers, archpriests, and scholars sat in council for a long time but could not think of what to do with him; they could not bring themselves to kill him.

Then one of them, Caiaphas, who in that year was the high priest, came up with this. He said to them: "It must be remembered that it is practical to kill one man so that an

117

entire nation will not perish. If we leave this man alone, the people as a nation will perish; this I predict to you, and so it is better to kill Jesus. Even if the people do not perish, they will nonetheless scatter and depart from the one faith if we do not kill Jesus; therefore, it is better to kill him."

And when Caiaphas said this, they all decided that there was nothing to discuss further and that Jesus must certainly be killed. They would have taken Jesus and killed him at that very moment, but he was hiding from them in the wilderness.

But at that time, the Passover holiday was approaching, and many people always went to Jerusalem for the holiday. The preachers and archpriests counted on Jesus' coming with the people for Passover. And so they announced to the people that if anyone should see Jesus, he should bring him to them.

And exactly six days before Passover, Jesus said to his disciples: "Let us go to Jerusalem." And he went with them.

And the disciples said to him: "Do not go to Jerusalem." And Jesus said to them: "I cannot fear anything because I live in the light of the enlightenment. And just as any man may walk in the daytime and not at night in order not to stumble, so any man may live by the enlightenment in order not to doubt or fear anything. Only he who lives by the flesh has doubts and fears, but there is nothing doubtful or terrible for him who lives by the enlightenment."

And Jesus came to the village of Bethany, near Jerusalem, to see Mary and Martha, and there the sisters made a supper for him. And when he sat down to supper, Martha served him, but Mary took a pound of expensive, undiluted, fragrant oil and spread it over Jesus' feet and dried them with her hair. And when the fragrance of the oil spread throughout the chamber, Judas Iscariot said: "Mary has wasted this expensive oil for nothing. It would have been better to sell the oil for three hundred coins and give it to the poor."

But Jesus said: "The poor will always be with you, but soon

I shall no longer be with you. She has done well; she has prepared my body for burial."

In the morning, Jesus went to Jerusalem. Many people were there for the holiday. And when they recognized Jesus, they gathered around him, broke branches from the trees, and threw their garments on the road before him. And they all shouted: "Here is our true king, the one who has taught us the true God." Jesus sat down on an ass and rode on it, while the people ran in front of him and cried out. And when he thus rode into the city, all the people became troubled and asked: "Who is this?" And those who knew him answered: "It is Jesus, the prophet from Nazareth, in Galilee."

And Jesus entered the temple and again drove out all the buyers and sellers.

And the preachers and archpriests saw all this and said to each other: "Look at what this man is doing. All the people follow him."

But they did not dare to take him away from the people openly, because they saw the people clinging to him, and they devised a way to take him by stealth.

Meanwhile, Jesus was in the temple teaching the people. Besides the Jews, there were Greek pagans among the people. The Greeks listened to the teaching of Jesus and realized that his teaching offered truth, and so they too wanted to be his disciples. And they spoke of this to Philip, and Philip told Andrew. The disciples were afraid to bring Jesus and the Greeks together. They were afraid that the people might grow embittered toward Jesus for not acknowledging the differences between Hebrews and other peoples, and for a long time they could not make up their minds to tell Jesus.

Once he heard that the Greeks wanted to be his disciples, Jesus said: "I know that the people will hate me for not drawing distinctions between the Jews and the pagans and for regarding myself as I would a pagan, but now the time has come when the teaching of the Son of God must be recognized among all peoples. And even if I perish for it, I must speak the truth. A grain of wheat brings forth fruit only when it dies. He who fears for the life of the flesh loses the true life, but he who despises the life of the flesh transforms this temporal life into a truth beyond time, in God."

And turning to Andrew and Philip, he said: "Let him who wants to serve my teaching do as I do. He who does what I do will be loved by my Father. Now it must be decided whether my life is to be carnal or spiritual. Now that the thing I have been approaching has come, am I to say, 'Father, deliver me from what I must do'? I cannot say that, for I have been moving toward it. And so I say, 'Father! Reveal yourself in me!'"

And turning to all the people, Jesus said: "Only in the present is the power of the spirit over the flesh to be found; only in the present is the power of the flesh defeated. And as I rise above earthly life, I shall draw everyone unto me."

And they said unto him: "We have heard, according to the law, that the Christ is something special and definite, something that always remains the same; how is it, then, that you, the Christ, are to rise up as the Son of man? What does it mean to raise up the Son of man?"

At this Jesus answered: "Raising up the Son of man means living by that light of the enlightenment that is in you; raising up the Son of man above the earthly means believing in the light of the enlightenment as long as the enlightenment exists, so that you may be a son of the enlightenment. He who believes in my teaching believes not in me but in the spirit that has given life to the world. My teaching is the very light of life that summons people from darkness. And if someone hears my words and does not fulfill them, I am not the one to condemn him, since my teaching does not condemn but saves. He who does not accept my words is condemned not by my teaching but by the enlightenment within him. This is what condemns him. For I have not spoken my own words but those with which my Father, the spirit living within me, has inspired me. What I speak is what the spirit of the enlightenment has spoken to me. And what I teach is the true life." Having said this, Jesus left and once again hid from the archpriests.

Among those who heard these words of Jesus were many rich and powerful people who believed in the teaching of Jesus but were afraid to acknowledge it before the archpriests; for not one of the archpriests had affirmed that he believed. For they judged according to the human and not the divine.

After Jesus had again gone into hiding, the archpriests and elders gathered once more in the courtyard of Caiaphas and began to devise a way to take Jesus secretly from the people and kill him. They were afraid to seize him openly. And one of the first twelve disciples of Jesus, Judas Iscariot, came to counsel with them and said: "If you want to take Jesus secretly, so that the people will not see, then I shall find a time when only a few people will be with him, and I shall show you where he is; then you can take him. What will you give me for this?" They promised him thirty rubles. He agreed, and from then on he began to seek a time to take the archpriests to Jesus so they could seize him.

Meanwhile, Jesus hid from the people, and only his disciples were with him. When the first day of the Feast of the Unleavened Bread came, the disciples said to Jesus: "Where shall we celebrate Passover?" And Jesus said: "Go some place in the village and stop in on someone there and say that you do not have time to prepare for Passover; ask him to allow us to celebrate Passover." The disciples did as they were told. They asked this of a certain man in the village, and he let them in.

Thus, they came and sat down at the table. Jesus knew

that Judas Iscariot had already promised to hand him over to death. But he did not expose Judas or take revenge on him for this; instead, just as he had taught love to his disciples with his whole life, so now he reproached Judas in love.

When all twelve of them were sitting at the table, he looked at them and said: "Among you sits one who has betrayed me. Yes, he who eats and drinks with me will destroy me."

They did not know of whom he spoke and began to have their supper. As they were getting ready to eat, Jesus took a piece of bread, broke it into twelve parts, gave each of the disciples a piece, and said: "Take, eat. If the one who is betraying me eats this bread, he will be eating my body." Then he poured some wine into a cup, gave it to the disciples, and said: "Drink, all of you, from this cup." And when they all had drunk, he said: "He who will betray me has drunk my blood. I pour out my blood so that people may know my testament—to forgive others their sins. I shall soon die and shall be with you no more in this world but shall be united with you only in God."

And after this, Jesus rose from the table, girded himself with a towel, took a pitcher of water, and began to wash the feet of all the disciples. He went up to Peter, and Peter said: "How is it that you are about to wash my feet?" Jesus said to him: "It seems strange to you that I wash your feet, but soon you will know why I do this. I do it because not all of you are clean, but my betrayer is among you, whose feet I want to wash."

And when Jesus had washed all their feet, he again sat down and said: "Have you understood why I have done this? I did it so that you too might do the same for one another. If I, your teacher, do this, then you must serve everyone all the more and not hate anyone. If you know this, then you are blessed. I do not speak of all of you but of one of you, whose feet I have washed and who has eaten bread with me; one of you will destroy me."

After saying this, Jesus grew troubled in spirit and confirmed that one of them would betray him. Again the disciples began to look around at one another and did not know of whom he spoke. One disciple sitting near Jesus, Simon Peter, motioned to him to ask who the betrayer was. And he asked. Jesus said: "I shall dip a piece of bread, and the one to whom I give it is the betrayer." And he gave it to Judas Iscariot and said to him: "What you want to do, do quickly." Judas understood that he had to leave, and as soon as he took the piece of bread, he left; it was not possible to chase after him because it was night.

And when Judas had gone, Jesus said: "Now it is clear to you what the Son of man is; now it is clear to you that he is in God, that he can forgive his enemies and do good. Children, I shall not be with you much longer. As I have told the preachers, do not philosophize about my teaching, but do as I do. I give you one new commandment: As I have loved you and the betrayer Judas, so love you one another. This alone distinguishes you; only in loving one another are you to be distinguished from other people."

And after this, they set out for the Mount of Olives. Along the way Jesus said to them: "The time is nearing when what is written in the Scriptures will come to pass: the shepherd will be killed, and all the sheep will run away. It will happen on this very night. They will take me, and all of you will abandon me and run away." And in answer to this, Peter said to him: "Even if all are frightened and run away, I shall not deny you. I am ready to go to my death with you."

Jesus said to him: "I say unto you that on this very night, before the cock crows, you will deny me not once but three times." But Peter said he would not deny him, and so said all the disciples.

And then, having seen that all the disciples were with him, Jesus met with a temptation. It hurt him that people wanted to kill him for no reason. And he said to the disciples: "At first, neither you nor I needed anything. You went around without a coin and without spare shoes, as I told you to do, but now that I am viewed as a criminal, this can no longer be so. You must equip yourselves with everything, arm yourselves with knives, so that you will not be destroyed for nothing." And the disciples said: "Here, we have two knives." And Jesus said: "Very well."

And they went beyond the river Kedron, where there was a garden, and they entered the garden.

And Jesus said to the disciples: "I have grown weak and must pray; be with me." And he seated Peter and the two Zebedees near him, and he began to groan and grieve that he had fallen into temptation and wanted to struggle against evil. He said: "It is painful and burdensome for me; help me; raise up the spirit together with me." And he fell to his knees and prayed. He said: "Father, my spirit, you are free. Give me strength, so that the struggle with temptation may leave me; so that everything may be as you will it, and not as I want it, so that I may join with your will." The disciples did not pray but were disheartened, and Jesus reproached them and said: "Pray, strengthen yourselves in spirit, so that you do not fall into the temptation of timidity and struggle. Strength lies in the soul, but the body is powerless." And for a second time, he began to pray and said: "Father, spirit, let everything be as you wish." Once more the disciples did not pray with him and grew dejected. And he prayed again, for a third time, and then, strengthened in spirit, he said to the disciples: "Soon, now, I shall be turned over into the hands of worldly people."

Chapter Eleven

THE FAREWELL DISCOURSE

PERSONAL LIFE is a deception of the flesh. The true life is the life common to all people.

When Jesus felt prepared for death and went to hand himself over, Peter stopped him and asked: "Where are you going?" Jesus answered: "I go where you cannot go. I am ready for death, but you are not yet prepared for it." Peter said: "No, I am ready now to give my life for you." Jesus answered: "Man cannot promise anything." And he said to all the disciples: "I know that death lies in wait for me, but I believe in the life of the Father, and so I do not fear it. Do not be troubled by my death but believe in the true God and in the Father of life, and then my death will not seem terrible to you. If I am joined with the Father of life, then I cannot lose my life. True, I do not tell you how or when or where my life will be after death, but I show you the way to the true life. My teaching does not speak of what sort of life it will be, but it reveals the one true way of life. It lies in the union with the Father; the Father is the origin of life. My teaching lies in living in the will of the Father and fulfilling his will for the sake of life and for the blessedness of all

125

people. After me, your mentor will be your consciousness of the truth. Fulfilling my teaching, you will always feel that you are in the truth, that the Father is in you and you are in the Father. And in the consciousness of the Father of life within you, you will experience the peace that nothing can take away from you. Thus, if you know the truth and live in it, neither my death nor your own can trouble you. People imagine themselves to be separate beings, each with his own will to life, but this is a deception. There is but one true life, the one that acknowledges the will of the Father as the origin of life. My teaching reveals this oneness of life and portrays life not as separate shoots but as a single tree on which all the shoots grow. Only he who lives in the will of the Father, as a shoot on the tree, truly lives, but he who wants to live according to his own will dies like a broken shoot. If you live in the will of the Father, you will have everything you desire, for life is given to people for the sake of blessedness. The Father has given me life for the sake of blessedness, and I have taught you to live for the sake of blessedness. If you fulfill my commandments, you will be blessed. The commandment that expresses the whole of my teaching is that people should love one another. And love consists of sacrificing your carnal life for the sake of another life. There is no other definition of love. And fulfilling my commandment of love, you will fulfill it not as slaves, who carry out their master's orders without understanding, but you will live as free people, just as I do; for I have explained to you the meaning of life that flows from the consciousness of the Father of life. You have accepted my teaching not because you just happened to choose it, but because it alone is true and it alone sets people free.

"The teaching of the world consists of doing evil to people, but my teaching lies in loving one another. And so the world will hate you, just as it has hated me.

"The world does not understand my teaching, and so it will

persecute you and do evil unto you, that it may thus serve
God; do not be surprised at this, and understand that this is
how it must be. Failing to understand the true God, the
world must drive you out, but you must affirm the truth. You
will grieve over their killing me, yet they kill me because of my
affirmation of the truth. Thus, my death is necessary for the
affirmation of the truth. My death, in the face of which I do
not abandon the truth, will confirm you, and you will realize
where is the lie and where the truth and what issues from the
knowledge of life and truth.

"You will realize that the lie is rooted in people's belief in
the life of the flesh and in their failure to believe in the life of
the spirit, that the truth is rooted in a union with the Father,
and that from this comes the victory of the spirit over the
flesh. When I am no longer in this carnal life, my spirit will
be with you. But you, like all people, will not always feel the
power of the spirit within you. Sometimes you will grow weak
and lose the power of the spirit, and you will fall into temptation; at other times, you will once again awaken to the true
life. The enslavement of the flesh will be upon you, but this
will be only for a while; you will suffer for a time, and then
you will be reborn through the spirit, like a woman who
suffers the torment of childbirth and then feels joy for having
borne a human being into the world. You will feel the same
when, after the enslavement of the flesh, you rise up through
the spirit: then you will feel such blessedness that you will
desire nothing else.

"Know this beforehand, and despite persecutions and the
inner struggle and breakdown of the spirit, know that the
spirit is alive within you and that the one true God is
the enlightenment of the will of the Father, which is revealed
by me." And turning to the Father-spirit, Jesus said: "I have
done what you have commanded me to do; I have revealed to
people that you are the origin of all things, and they have

understood me. I have taught them that they all issue from the one source of eternal life and that they are therefore all one, that just as the Father is in me and I am in the Father, so are they one with me and with the Father. I have revealed to them that just as you have sent them into the world in love, so must they live in the world through love."

AND PETER SAID TO JESUS: "Where are you going?" Jesus answered: "You do not have the strength to go where I am going now; only afterward will you go there."

And Peter said: "Why do you think that I do not have the strength to go now to where you are going? I shall give my life for you." And Jesus said: "You say you will give your life for me, but before the cock crows, you will deny me three times."

And Jesus said to the disciples: "Do not be troubled and do not grow timid, but believe in the true God of life and in my teaching. The life of the Father is not the only one here on earth, but there is another life. If there were only life as it is here, I would have told you that when I die I would enter into the bosom of Abraham and there prepare a place for you, and that I would come and take you and together we would be blessed in the bosom of Abraham. But I show you only the path to life."

Thomas said: "But we do not know where you are going, and so we cannot know the way. We must know what will be after death." Jesus said: "I cannot show you what will be there; my teaching is the way, the truth, and the life. There is no other way to be united with the Father of life except through my teaching. If you fulfill my teaching, then you will know the Father."

Philip said: "But who is the Father?" Jesus said: "The Father is that which gives life. I have fulfilled the will of the Father; thus, according to my life, you may realize what the will of the Father consists of. I live through the Father, and the Father lives in me; and everything I say and do, I do according to the will of the Father. My teaching lies in the fact that I am in the Father and the Father is in me. If you do not understand the teaching itself, then behold me and my deeds, and then you will be able to understand what the Father is. And you know that whoever follows my teaching can do as I do and even more, since I shall die but he will yet live. He who lives by my teaching will have all he desires, for then the son will be the same as the Father.

"Whatever you desire according to my teaching, you will have.

"But for this, one must love my teaching. My teaching will provide you with an intercessor and a comforter in my place. The comforter will be an awareness of the truth, which worldly people do not comprehend, but you will know it in yourselves. You will never be alone if the spirit of my teaching is within you. I shall die and worldly people will not see me, but you will see me because my teaching lives and you will live through it. Then, if my teaching is within you, you will understand that I am in the Father and the Father is in me. He who fulfills my teaching will feel the Father within himself, and in this, my spirit will live."

And Judas—not Iscariot but another—said to him: "But why cannot everyone live according to the spirit of truth?" And in answer to this, Jesus said: "Only he who fulfills my teaching loves the Father, and only in him can my spirit be implanted. He who does not fulfill my teaching cannot love my Father, for the teaching is not mine but the Father's. That is all I can tell you now. But my spirit, the spirit of truth that after me will take root in you, will reveal everything to you, and you will remember and understand much of what I have said to you.

"Then you may always be at peace in spirit, and not with the worldly calm that people of the world seek but with the tranquillity of spirit, so that through it you will no longer fear anything. In the light of this, if you fulfill my teaching, then my death will in no way cause you sorrow. I shall come to you as the spirit of truth, and together with the consciousness of the Father, I shall be implanted in your heart. If you fulfill my teaching, then you must rejoice, for in my place, the Father will be with you in your heart, and this is better for you.

"My teaching is the tree of life. The Father is the one who cultivates the tree. He cleans and tends to the branches on which there is fruit, so that they may bring forth more.

"Hold to my teaching of life, and life will be in you. And just as the shoot lives not of itself but from the tree, so will you live from my teaching. My teaching is the tree, and you are the shoots. He who lives by my teaching of life brings forth much fruit, and apart from my teaching, there is no life. Whoever does not live by my teaching withers and dies, and the dry branches will be cut off and burned. If you live by my teaching and fulfill it, then you will have all you desire. For it is the will of the Father that you live the true life and have what you desire. Just as the Father has given me the good, so do I give you the good. Hold to this good. I live because the Father loves me and I love the Father, and you must live by that same love. If you live by this, then you will be blessed. My commandment is that you love one another as I love you. There is no greater love than this, that we sacrifice ourselves out of love for others, just as I have done.

"Love one another, for love is from God. And he who loves is born from God and knows God. But he who does not love does not know God, for God is love. God's love for us is shown in this, that he has sent his son, such as he himself, into the world so that we may live through him.

"His love for us may be seen in the fact that we have not loved God, yet he has loved us, and we must love one another.

God is never seen. If we love one another, God abides within us, and his love is consummated in us. We recognize each other only in this, that we abide in him and he in us, that he has bestowed his spirit upon us.

"Love is consummated within us when we are assured and at peace on the day of our death, for just as God is, so are we in this world. Love does not know fear; on the contrary, perfect love destroys fear, because from fear comes altercation, struggle. And he who fears is not perfect in his love.

"We love God only because he has loved us first. (Therefore we first know love for people.) And so if someone says, 'I love God, but I shall not love my brother,' he lies, for he who does not love his brother, whom he sees, cannot love God, whom he has not seen and does not see. The commandment to love God is a commandment to love your brother.

"You are my equal if you do what I have taught you. I do not consider you slaves, who are ordered, but equals, for I have explained to you everything I have understood about the Father. You have not chosen my teaching according to your own will but because I have shown you the one truth, before which you may live and have all you desire. The whole teaching lies in loving one another. Do not be surprised if the world should hate you; it hates my teaching. If you were of the world, it would love you. But I have separated you from the world, and for this it will despise you. If I am driven out, so will you be driven out.

"They will do all this because they do not know the true God. I have explained it to them, but they do not want to even listen to me. They have not understood the Father. They have seen my life, and my life has shown them their error. And for this, they have come to hate me even more. The spirit of truth that will come to you will also confirm this. And you will confirm it. I tell you this beforehand, so that you may not be deceived when you are persecuted. They will make you into apostates. Everyone will think that by killing you they are doing what is pleasing to God. They cannot help doing all this because they understand neither my teaching nor the true God. I tell you all this beforehand, so that you will not be surprised when it all happens.

"Thus, I now go off to the spirit who has sent me, and now you understand that you must not ask where I go. Before this, you were grieved that I did not tell you precisely where, to what sort of place, I am going. But verily I say unto you, it is good for you that I go away. If I do not die, then the spirit of truth will not appear to you, but if I die, then it will be implanted within you. The spirit will be implanted within you, and it will be clear to you as to what is a lie, what is truth, and what the resolution. The lie consists of the fact that people do not believe in the life of the spirit. The truth consists of the fact that I am one with the Father. The resolution consists of the fact that the power of the carnal life is destroyed.

"I could tell you much more, but it would be difficult for you to understand. When the spirit of truth is implanted within you, it will reveal to you the whole truth, for it will not tell you something new, from itself, but what is from God, and it will show you the way in all of life's circumstances. It too will be from the Father, as I am from the Father, for it will speak what I speak. But even when I, the spirit of truth, am in you, you will not always see me. Sometimes you will hear me, but at other times you will not."

And the disciples said to each other: "What does this mean, what he said, 'Sometimes you will see me, at other times you will not'? What does it mean, that sometimes it will be, at other times it will not be? What is he saying?" Jesus said to them: "You do not understand what this means, that sometimes you will see me, at other times you will not? You know how it always is in the world, that some are sad and mourn, while others rejoice. You too will be sad, but your sadness will be transformed into joy. When a woman is giving birth, she grieves over her torment, but when it is over, she does not remember her torment because of her joy at having brought a human being into the world.

"So too will you be sad, and suddenly you will see me, the spirit of truth will enter you, and your sadness will turn into joy. And then you will no longer ask anything of me, because then you will have all you desire. Then all one desires in spirit, he will have from his Father. Previously you asked for nothing for the sake of the spirit, but you will request what you want for the spirit, and everything will be yours, so that your blessedness may be complete. I, a man, cannot now express this to you in words, but when, as the spirit of truth, I live within you, I shall clearly proclaim the Father to you. Then everything you ask of the Father in the name of the spirit, not I but the Father will give to you, for he loves you because you have accepted my teaching. You have understood that the enlightenment from the Father arises in the world and returns from the world to the Father."

Then the disciples said to Jesus: "Now we have understood everything, and we have nothing more to ask. We believe that you are from God." And Jesus said: "I have told you all this so that you may have the assurance and peace of my teaching. No matter what misfortunes may befall you in the world, fear nothing; my teaching has conquered the world."

After this, Jesus lifted up his eyes toward heaven and said: "My Father, you have given your son the freedom of life, that he may know the true life. Life is the knowledge of the true God, the enlightenment revealed by me. I have revealed you to people on earth. I have done the work you commanded me to do. I have revealed your essence to people on earth. They were yours even before this, but according to your will, I have shown them the truth, and they have come to know you. They have realized that all they have, their very life, comes only from you. And what I have taught them is not from myself, but they and I arise from you. I pray to you for those who acknowledge you. They have realized that all that is mine is yours and all that is yours is mine. I am no longer in the world but am returning to you. Yet they are in the world, and so I pray to you, Father, keep your enlightenment in them. I do not ask you to take them from the world but to deliver them from evil. May they be confirmed in your truth. Your enlightenment is truth.

"My Father! I wish that they may be as I am; that they may understand, as I do, that the true life began before the beginning of the world; that they may all be one, as you, Father, are in me and I in you, all united as one; and that people may realize that they have not been born from themselves, but that you, loving them, have sent them into the world, as you have sent me.

"Righteous Father! The world has not known you, but I have known you. And I have explained to them what you are. You are this, that the love with which you have loved me may be in them. You have given them life, and so you have loved them. I have taught them to recognize this and to love you, so that your love for them may be returned to you from them."

Chapter Twelve

THE VICTORY OF THE SPIRIT

OVER THE FLESH

ND HAVING SAID THIS, Jesus set off with his disciples for the Garden of Gethsemane. And upon arriving at the garden, Jesus said: "Let us stay here; I want to pray." And as he approached Peter and the two Zebedee brothers, he began to grow weary and sad. And he said to them: "My heart is heavy; I grow sad at my death. Stay here and do not be as dejected as I am." And he went off a short distance, lay face down on the earth, and began to pray and said: "My Father, spirit, let it not be as I wish, that I should not die, but do as you wish: let me die. But for you, as spirit, all things are possible; so let me be not afraid of death, so there will be no temptations of the flesh for me."

And then he rose and went up to the disciples and saw that they had grown melancholy, and he said to them: "Do you not have the strength to be raised up by the spirit for one hour, that you may not fall into the temptations of the flesh? The spirit is strong, but the flesh is weak."

And again Jesus went off a short distance from them; again

he began to pray and said: "Father, if I must die, then let me die. May your will be done."

And having said this, he again went up to the disciples and saw that they were downcast and ready to weep. And once more he went off a short distance from them and for a third time said: "Father, may your will be done."

Then he returned to the disciples and said to them: "Sleep on now and rest, for the Son of man will be delivered into the hands of worldly people.

"Then awaken, for already the one who will betray me is coming."

And just as he said this, Judas, one of the disciples, suddenly showed up, and with him was a large crowd of people with clubs and knives.

Judas knew that Jesus often came to this garden with his disciples, and so he brought the guards and servants of the archpriests there. He said to them: "I shall take you there, where he is with his disciples. And so that you may recognize him from the others, look to see whom I kiss first; he will be the one." And he immediately went up to Jesus and said: "Hello, Teacher." And he kissed him. And Jesus said to him: "Did you come for this?" Then the guards surrounded Jesus and wanted to take him. At that, Peter took a knife from a servant of an archpriest and cut off his ear.

Jesus said: "We must not resist evil. Let it be." And he said to Peter: "Give the sword back to the one from whom you took it. He who takes up the sword will perish by the sword."

After that, Jesus turned to the crowd and said: "Why do you set upon me with weapons, as you would set upon a robber? After all, I have been among you every day in the temple and have taught you. Why did you not take me then? But in the light of day, you could do nothing to me; your strength lies only in the darkness." Then, seeing he would be taken, all the disciples fled.

Then the leader ordered the soldiers to seize Jesus and bind him; the soldiers bound him and took him first to the house of Annas, the father-in-law of Caiaphas. Caiaphas was the high priest that year and lived with his father-in-law. This was the same Caiaphas who had devised a way to destroy Jesus. He found it would be practical for the people to destroy Jesus, for if Jesus were not destroyed, things would be worse for the entire people.

And Jesus was brought to the courtyard of the house where the high priest lived.

As they took Jesus there, one of the disciples, Peter, followed him from afar and watched to see where they were taking him. When Jesus was brought into the courtyard of the high priest, Peter also went in to see how it would all come out. And a girl in the courtyard saw Peter and said to him: "Weren't you too with Jesus the Galilean?" Peter grew afraid that he might be accused and before all the people said in a loud voice: "I do not know what you are talking about!" Then, when Jesus was taken into the house and Peter went with the people into the vestibule, a woman was warming herself by the fire. Peter approached; the woman looked at Peter and said to the people: "Look, this man resembles one who was also with Jesus the Nazarene." Peter became more frightened still and swore that he had never been with Jesus and that he did not know this man Jesus. A short while later, some people came up to Peter and said: "But it is evident from everything that you too are one of these rebels; we can tell from your speech that you are from Galilee." Then Peter began to curse and swear that he had never known and had never seen Jesus.

And as soon as he said this, the cock crowed. And Peter remembered the words Jesus had spoken to him when Peter swore that even if everyone denied him, he would never deny him: "This night, before the cock crows, you will deny me three times." And Peter went out from the courtyard and wept bitterly.

Preachers, archpriests, scribes, and officials gathered at the house of the high priest. And when they were all assembled, Jesus was brought in, and the high priest asked him what his teaching consisted of and who his disciples were.

And Jesus replied: "I have always spoken and still speak in front of everyone, and I have never hidden, nor do I hide anything from anyone. What is it you are asking me about? Ask those who have heard and understood my teaching; they will tell you." When Jesus said this, one of the archpriests' servants struck him in the face and said: "Do you know with whom you are speaking? Is this the way to answer an archpriest?" Jesus said: "If I have spoken badly, then say that I have spoken badly. But if I did not speak badly, then why do you beat me?"

The preachers and archpriests tried to accuse Jesus and at first could find no evidence against him for which he might be condemned. Then they found two false witnesses. These false witnesses said of Jesus: "We ourselves heard how this man said: 'I shall destroy your handmade temple, and in three days, I shall build another temple to God that is not made with hands.'"

But even this evidence was not enough to accuse him. And so an archpriest called Jesus out and said: "Why do you not reply to their testimony?" Jesus was silent and said nothing. Then the archpriest said to him: "Well, then, tell me, are you the Christ, the Son of God?" Jesus answered him and said: "Yes, I am the Christ, the Son of God. And you yourselves will soon see that the Son of man is equal to God." Then the archpriest cried out: "You blaspheme God, and now we need no further evidence; now we have all heard that you are a blasphemer." And the archpriest turned to the assembly and said: "Now you yourselves have heard him blaspheme God; to what do you sentence him for this?" And they all said: "We sentence him to death." And then all the people and the guards, everyone, fell upon Jesus and began to spit in his face and strike him on the cheeks and scratch him. They covered his eyes, beat him in the face, and said: "Well, now, you are a prophet, so guess who is hitting you!" And Jesus was silent.

After they reviled him, they bound him and took him to Pontius Pilate.

And he was taken to the seat of government. Pilate, the governor, came out to see him and asked: "Of what do you accuse this man?" They said: "This man does evil, and that is why we have brought him to you." And Pilate said to them: "If he has done you evil, then judge him yourselves according to your law." But they said: "We have brought him to you for you to execute him, since we are not allowed to kill him." Thus, what Jesus had wished came to pass: he had said that he must be prepared to die on the cross at the hands of the Romans, and not by his own hand or at the hands of the Jews.

And when Pilate asked them what they accused him of, they said that he was guilty of inciting the people to rebellion, of forbidding people to pay taxes to Caesar, and of setting himself up as Christ and king. Pilate heard them out and ordered Jesus to be brought before him in the court. When Jesus came to him, Pilate asked: "Are you the King of the Jews?" Jesus said: "What are you asking? Is it for yourself that you ask whether or not I am King of the Jews, or are you asking if what they have told you about me is true?" Pilate said: "I am not a Jew, and I do not care what you call yourself; I am only asking what you have done. Have you called yourself a king?" Jesus answered: "I have taught a kingdom that is not of the earth. If I were an earthly king, my subjects would fight for me and would not yield to the archpriests, and so you see that my kingdom is not of the earth." To this Pilate said: "Do you nevertheless consider yourself a king?" Jesus said:

"Not only I but you too cannot help but consider me a king. I teach only in order to reveal to you the truth. And anyone who lives by the truth will understand me." Pilate did not want to listen to Jesus and said: "You speak of truth; what is truth?" And having said this, he turned and went back to the archpriests and said to them: "In my view, this man has done nothing wrong."

But the archpriests persisted and said that he had done much evil and incited the people to rebellion and created rebellion in all Judea, as far as Galilee. Then Pilate again began to interrogate Jesus in front of the archpriests, but Jesus did not answer. "Do you not see how they accuse you? Why do you not justify yourself?" But Jesus still remained silent and said not a word, so that Pilate was amazed at him.

Pilate recalled that Galilee was under King Herod's jurisdiction and asked: "Is he from Galilee?" They told him yes. Then he said: "If he is from Galilee, then he is under Herod's jurisdiction; I am sending him to Herod." At that time, Herod was in Jerusalem, and in order to get rid of Jesus, Pilate sent him to Jerusalem to see Herod. When Jesus was brought to Herod, Herod was very glad to see Jesus. He had heard much about him and wanted to find out what sort of man he was. He summoned him and began to question him about everything he wanted to know, but Jesus answered nothing. And the archpriests and teachers harshly accused Jesus before Herod, as they had before Pilate, and said that he was a rebel. And Herod regarded Jesus as a worthless man; to mock him, he ordered him to be dressed in a red robe and sent him back to Pilate.

Herod was satisfied that Pilate was showing him respect by sending Jesus to be judged by him, and so they were reconciled, for they had previously been at odds. When Jesus was once more brought to him, Pilate again summoned the archpriests and the Jewish officials and said to them: "You have brought me this man because he incites the people to rebellion; I have questioned him in your presence, and I do not see that he is a rebel. I sent him with you to Herod, and you see that there too nothing harmful about him was found; in my view, there is no reason to condemn him to death, and it would be better not to punish him but to release him."

And when the archpriests heard this, they all shouted: "No! Execute him, execute him in Roman style: crucify him on the cross!" Pilate listened and said to the archpriests: "Very well, but you have a custom for the Passover feast to pardon one criminal. I have here in prison a certain Barabbas, a murderer and a rebel. One of them, then, must be released; whom will you pardon—Jesus or Barabbas?" Pilate wanted to spare Jesus, but the archpriests stirred up the people, so that everyone cried: "Barabbas! Barabbas!" and Pilate said: "But what is to be done with Jesus?" And again they shouted: "To the cross, Roman style, to the cross with him!" And Pilate began to urge them to do otherwise, saying: "Why are you so against him? He has done nothing to be condemned to death, nor has he done you any evil. I shall release him, for I find no guilt in him." The archpriests and their servants shouted: "Crucify him, crucify him!" And Pilate said to them: "If that is how it is, then take him and crucify him yourselves. But I see no guilt in him." The archpriests answered: "We demand what is coming to him for making himself out to be the Son of God."

When Pilate heard these words, he was troubled because he did not know what the words meant: the Son of God. He returned to the court, and once more Pilate summoned Jesus and asked him: "Who are you, and where do you come from?" But Jesus did not answer him. Then Pilate said: "Why do you not answer me? Can you not see that you are in my power and that I can either crucify you or let you go?" Jesus replied to him: "The whole evil lies in your having power; if you were not entrusted with power, the Herodians would not tease you and lead you into temptation, both you and the teachers with you." Pilate wanted to release Jesus, but the Jews said to him: "If you release Jesus, then by this you will show that you are not a faithful servant of Caesar, because he who makes himself into a king is the enemy of Caesar." And when Pilate heard these words, he realized that he could not avoid executing Jesus.

Then Pilate went out to the Jews, took some water, washed his hands in front of the people, and said: "I am not guilty of the blood of this righteous man." And all the people shouted: "Let his blood be upon us and upon our children!"

Thus, the archpriests prevailed. Then Pilate sat down in the seat of judgment and ordered Jesus first to be flogged. As he was being flogged, the soldiers who were flogging him placed a crown on his head and a stick in his hands; they threw a red robe over his back and began to jeer at him. They bowed at his feet in mockery and said: "Rejoice, King of the Jews." Then they struck him on the cheeks and head and spit in his face.

And Pilate said to them: "How can you want to crucify your king?" But the archpriests cried: "Crucify him! Our king is Caesar, crucify him!"

Jesus came out in the crown and red robe and said: "Here is the man."

Then Pilate sentenced him to be crucified.

Then they took the red garment from Jesus, placed his own coat on him, and ordered him to carry the cross to the place called Golgotha in order to be crucified there. And he carried the cross and thus came to the place called Golgotha. And there they stretched Jesus out (crucified him) on the cross and two other men with him; the two were on each side and Jesus in the middle.

As they were crucifying him, Jesus said: "Father, forgive

them; they do not know what they do." And when Jesus was hanging on the cross, the people surrounded him and cursed at him.

They came up, nodded their heads toward him, and said: "Well, you wanted to destroy the temple in Jerusalem and build it again in three days, so save yourself and come down from the cross!" And the archpriests and preachers stood there and mocked him and said: "He saved others, but he cannot save himself. Show us you are the Christ: come down from the cross, and then we shall believe you. He said he was the Son of God and that God would not forsake him; so why has God forsaken him now?"

And the people, the archpriests, and the soldiers cursed at him, and even one of the thieves who were crucified with him cursed at him.

Cursing him, one of the thieves said: "If you are the Christ, then save yourself and us too." But the other thief heard this and said: "Have you no fear of God? You yourself are on the cross, and you curse an innocent man. You and I are being executed for our deeds, but this man has done nothing wrong." And turning to Jesus, this thief said: "Lord, remember me in your kingdom." And Jesus said to him: "Even now you are blessed with me."

At the ninth hour, exhausted, Jesus cried out in a loud voice: *"Eli, Eli, lama sabachthani?,"* which means, "My God, my God, why have you forsaken me?" And when the people heard this, they began to talk and laugh: "He is calling the prophet Elijah; let us see how Elijah will come." Then Jesus uttered: "I thirst." And a man took a sponge, dipped it into a vat of vinegar that stood there, and raised it up to Jesus on a reed. Jesus sucked on the sponge and said in a loud voice: "It is finished. Father! Into your hands I commend my spirit." His head bowed, he gave up the spirit.

Conclusion to

THE INVESTIGATION OF THE GOSPEL

ITH THE WORDS "it is finished," the Gospel is also finished. For those who have seen the divinity of Jesus in his being unlike other people, his resurrection could have some cogency; that is, it could prove to them that he was unlike all other people, but only that he was unlike all other people, and nothing else. Only those who saw how Jesus died were convinced that he died; then they saw that he was alive and were convinced that he was alive. But according to the Gospel writers' description—with the exception of Luke, who suddenly mentions his ascension in front of five hundred men—there were no such people; according to the description, he appeared as in a dream, as in a vision.

But let us suppose that he did appear in the flesh and that Thomas put a finger into his wounds; what did this prove to Thomas? That Jesus was not the same sort of man as others. But what follows from the fact that Jesus was not the same sort of man as others? Only that it is very hard or impossible for people who are like everyone else to do what an utterly special being has done. But even if it were necessary to con-

144

vince people that he was not like other men, his appearance to Thomas and ten others and then to five hundred could in no way convince those who had not seen this resurrection. Only the disciples talked about a resurrection, but one can talk about anything; in order to believe the disciples' tales, the truth of their tales must somehow be confirmed. Thus, in order to confirm the truth of their tale, the disciples relate that tongues of fire descended upon them and that they themselves performed miracles, healed, and raised from the dead. The fact that tongues of fire descended upon them and that the disciples healed and raised from the dead is further confirmed by the disciples' disciples through yet new miracles, and so up to our time's relics and saints' healing and raising from the dead. Thus, it turns out that the divinity of Christ is based on the tales of unusual events. The tales of unusual events, in turn, are based on tales of other unusual events, yet the last of the unusual events have not been seen by people of sound mind. Very well. Christ was resurrected, showed himself, and flew off to heaven; does the reason for his doing this explain anything? Has it added anything to his teaching? Nothing, absolutely nothing, except the need to think up new unnecessary miracles in order to confirm this contrived, unnecessary miracle. We have seen, have read, and now read the teaching on the life of Christ prior to his resurrection, and in the most perverted passages of this teaching shines everywhere the light of the truth that he announced to the world. No matter how crudely the recording Gospel writers understand the teaching, they convey the words and actions of the man Jesus, and the light staggers us. What, indeed, is added to the teaching after the resurrection? What did Christ do and say after the resurrection?

He appeared for some reason to Mary Magdalene, from whom he cast out seven devils, and told her not to touch him, for he had not yet entered into the Father.

Then he appeared to other women and said he would come to see his brothers.

Then he appeared to the disciples and explained something to them from Moses about the whole Scripture.

And now they see him, and now they don't. Then he appeared to the disciples, reproached them for not believing, showed them his side, and breathed on them. And from this, it is supposed to happen that he whose sins they forgive is forgiven. Then he appeared to Thomas, and again he said nothing. Then he caught a fish; indeed, he caught many fish with his disciples and fried them. And three times he said to Peter, "Feed my sheep," and he foretold Peter's death. Then he appeared to five hundred brothers all at once and there too said nothing. Then he said he had been given power over heaven and earth; that therefore it is necessary to bathe people in the name of the Father and the Son and the Holy Spirit; and that whoever is thus bathed is saved. And that those to whom this spirit is transmitted will take snakes in their hands and drink poison without harm and speak in all languages, which they obviously have not done and do not do. And then he flew off to heaven. He said nothing more. Why was there a resurrection, if it was only to do and say this foolishness?

And so: 1. Like any story about something that cannot be understood, the resurrection cannot prove anything.

2. The resurrection, like any miracle someone may have seen, can prove only that something contrary to laws of reason has occurred and that the person subjected to the miracle has been subjected to something unusual, and nothing more. But if, on the basis of the miracle, it is concluded that a man who is not subject to the laws of reason is an unusual man, then this conclusion is correct only for those who contemplate the miracle and only while they are contemplating it. The tale of the miracle can convince no one, so that the truth must be

confirmed by a miracle that has happened to the teller of the tale. The confirmation of the truth of the miracle through a miracle inevitably entails for the confirmation of the story-teller's truth the invention of new miracles up to our own times, in which we clearly see that there are no miracles; just as the miracle of our day is fabricated, so must the miracle of the past have been fabricated. The story of the miracle of Christ's resurrection can be seen to abound in falsehood mostly by the fact that this story differs sharply from all the previous description of the life of Christ in its baseness, its insignificance, and its sheer stupidity. It clearly shows that the story of the real life of Christ had for its foundation an actual life full of depth and holiness, but the story of the resurrection and the imaginary actions and words that followed it had no foundation in life and is a complete fabrication. No matter how crude and base the description of the life of Christ may be, the holiness of Christ's life and the eminence of his personality shine through the crudeness and baseness of the writers. But when there is no longer anything real at the base of the description but only mere fabrication, then the crudeness and baseness appear in all their nakedness. It is evident that they had resurrected something of a resurrection, but they have not been able to make him say and do anything that is worthy of him.

3. The miracle of the resurrection is directly opposed to the teaching of Christ; thus, it was difficult to make Jesus say something in keeping with his nature after the resurrection, since the very idea that he could be resurrected is in direct contradiction to the whole meaning of his teaching. One would have to completely misunderstand his teaching to speak of his resurrection in the body. He even denied resurrection outright, explaining how the resurrection of which the Jews spoke must be understood.

How the dead are awakened, he told them (Luke 20:37),

Moses showed in the bush, when he called God the God of Abraham, the God of Isaac, and the God of Jacob; God is not the God of the dead but the God of the living. Because for God, all are alive. He said: I am the living bread sent down from heaven. He said: I am the way, the truth, and the life. And the one who thought that he was sent from God into the world to give life to people; the one who gives life; the one who is spirit; the one who does not die; the one who will return to people as the spirit of truth—this is the very one whom they understood to be resurrected in the body. Indeed, what could that Jesus do, who rejoiced in his return to the Father, that Jesus who said as he was dying, "Into your hands I commend my spirit"; what could he do and say when he was imagined to have been resurrected in the body, except what was obviously contradictory to his teaching? And so it was.

This legend of the resurrection related in the last chapter of the Gospel—which has no basis in the life and words of Christ but belongs solely to the views of the recorders of the Gospels regarding the life and teaching of Jesus—is remarkable and instructive in that these chapters clearly show the thickness of the layers of misunderstanding that cover up the whole description of the life and teaching of Jesus. It is as if a valuable painting had been smeared over with layers of paint, and those spots where the paint fell onto the bare wall clearly revealed the thickness of the layers covering the painting. The story of the resurrection provides the key to understanding and explaining all the miracles that overflow the Gospels and those contradictory words and concepts that often destroy the meaning of the best passages in the teaching.

It is not known who wrote the fourth Gospel, and the history of criticism has already led to the conviction that we will never know. There can be more or less probable suggestions about time, place, and persons; there can be propositions about what parts of which Gospels were copied from another Gospel; but their origin is unknown. We cannot judge the historical truth of the Gospel, but we can judge the virtues of the books themselves. We can judge what served as the basis for people's Christian beliefs and what had no influence on those beliefs.

In this regard, we see in the Gospels two sharply differing portions of the accounts: one is the account of the teaching, and the other is to prove the truth of the teaching or, rather, to prove the importance of the teaching, through such things as miracles, prophecies, and predictions. The teaching has traversed the centuries intact; everyone is agreed on this. The proofs that likely served as proofs now constitute the primary stumbling block to the reception of the teaching.

All the miracles belong to this part, and the chief miracle is the resurrection. In the description of the resurrection, as with any event fabricated without any foundation, it is easiest to trace the methods for composing such legends, why they are accepted, the devices of the account, their significance, and the consequences. The origin of the legend of the resurrection was the verification of the truthfulness of the writers (excluding Luke), and it is noted in the Gospels themselves so clearly that any unbiased person cannot help seeing the most natural embryo of the legend, just as it is conceived all around us every day in the tales of the miracles of relics, ascetics, and magicians. The stories and articles about spiritualism, about the girl who materialized and danced, are told much more definitely and affirmatively than the story of the resurrection. The history of the origin of this legend is as clear as can be. On the Sabbath, they went to see the tomb. There was no body. The Gospel writer John himself relates that it was said that the disciples took the body away. Women go to the tomb; one of them is Mary Magdalene, from whom seven devils had been cast out, and she is the first to relate that she saw something at the tomb, maybe a gardener, maybe an angel, maybe Jesus himself. The story passes from one gossip to another and then to the disciples. Eighty years later, it is told that such and such a person saw him here and there, but all the stories are confused and indefinite. None of the disciples invented them—this is obvious—but none of the people honoring his memory dares to contradict what, in that person's view, adds to his glory and, above all, to convince others that he is from God and that God created a sign in his honor. They think this is the best proof, and so the legend grows and spreads.

The legend promotes the promulgation of the teaching, but the legend is a lie, while the teaching is the truth. Hence, the teaching is transmitted not in the purity of truth but is confused with a lie. The lie summons a lie for its confirmation. New false legends of miracles are told to confirm the first false legend. Legends arise concerning the miracles of Christ's followers and miracles that preceded him—his conception, his birth, his whole life—and the teaching is mixed with lies. All the accounts of his life and teaching are covered with a crude layer of paint made of the miraculous, which obscures the teaching. New believers join the faith of Christ not so much because of his teaching as because of the miraculous nature of his life and deeds. And a terrible time comes when the concept of faith is not *pistis,* the faith of which Christ speaks (the inward inevitability of conviction that becomes the basis of life), but faith as the consequence of an effort of the will, whereby one may say: I command you to believe, I want you to believe, you must believe. The time comes when all the false legends replace the teaching, all gathered into one, formulated and expressed as "dogma," that is, as decrees. The crowd, the crude crowd, takes possession of the teaching and, after smearing it over with false legends, obscures it.

But in spite of all the power of the crowd, selected people

see the truth through all the filth of the lie and carry it through the centuries in all its purity and strength right next to the lie, and in such a form, the teaching reaches us. He who now, in our time, reads the Gospel finds himself in a strange position, whether he is Catholic, Protestant, Orthodox, Molokan, Stundist, Khlyst, Skopets, Rationalist, or any other creed. He who refuses to close his eyes cannot help seeing that, while not everything is here that we know and live by, there is at least something very wise and significant. But this wisdom and importance are expressed so hideously, so badly, as Goethe says, that one cannot find a book more poorly written than the Gospel; it is buried in such a trash heap of hideous, stupid, and even unpoetic legends, and the significant part is so inextricably bound to these legends, that you do not know what to do with this book. There are no interpretations of this book other than the ones that the various churches provide. These interpretations are all filled with absurdities and contradictions, so that one is initially presented with two ways out: either become furious with the lice and toss the whole coat into the fire, that is, reject the whole thing as nonsense, which is what ninety-nine out of a hundred do, or suppress your reason, which is what the Church orders us to do, and accept everything that is stupid and insignificant along with what is wise and significant. This is what one out of a hundred people do, those who either do not have the vsion or know how to squint so that they will not see what they do not want to see. Once these people are shown what they do not want to see, they automatically abandon not only the lie but the truth that was mixed in with it. And what is terrible about this is that the lie smeared in with the truth is often smeared in not by the enemies of the truth but by its closest friends. That this lie was considered important and was the first instrument in the spread and confirmation of the truth is shown by the fact that in the times of the apostles and martyrs of the first centuries, the lie concerning the resurrection of Christ was the primary proof of the truth of Christ's teaching. True, this very fable about the resurrection was also the main cause of nonbelief in the teaching. Throughout the lives of all the first Christian martyrs, the pagans called them people who believed their crucified one was resurrected, and they quite legitimately mocked this.

But the Christians did not see this, just as the popes in Kiev do not see that their relics stuffed with straw are, on the one hand, an encouragement of faith and, on the other hand, the chief obstacle to faith. Then, in the initial times of Christianity, it cannot be denied that these fables were needed; I am even prepared to agree that they promoted the spread and confirmation of the teaching. I can imagine that, thanks to the confidence in the miracle, people realized the importance of the teaching and turned to it. The miracle was not a proof of truth but a proof of the importance of the matter. The miracle drew attention; the miracle was an advertisement. Everything that happened was foretold: a voice speaks from heaven, the sick are healed, the dead are resurrected. How can one help but turn one's attention to the teaching and try to grasp it? Its truth penetrates into the soul, but the miracles are only an advertisement. Thus, the lie was useful. But it could be useful only in the initial times, useful only because it attracted people to the truth. If there had been no lie at all, perhaps the teaching would have spread even more rapidly. But it is pointless to judge what might have been. The lie concerning the miracles at that time may be compared with a man planting a forest, who places a sign on the site declaring that God planted the forest and that whoever does not believe there is a forest here will be eaten up by monsters. People might believe this and would not trample on the forest. This may have been useful and necessary in its time, when there was no forest, but when the forest grows up, it is obvious that what had been useful has become unnecessary and, like an untruth, has become harmful. So it is with faith in the miracles tied to the teaching; the belief in them helped the spread of the teaching, and they may have been useful. But the teaching has been spread and confirmed, and the belief in the miracles has become unnecessary and harmful. As long as the miracles and the lie were believed, it happened that the teaching itself was so confirmed that its confirmation and dissemination became the essential proof of its truth. The teaching has traversed the centuries intact; everyone is agreed on this. And the external, miraculous proofs of its truth constitute the primary stumbling block to the reception of the teaching. For us, the proofs of the truth and the importance of Christ's teaching now only interfere with seeing the significance of Christ.

Its existence for eighteen hundred years among billions of people sufficiently demonstrates for us its importance. Perhaps it was necessary to say that the forest was planted by God and that a monster guards it and God defends it; perhaps this was necessary when there was no forest, but now I have lived in the eighteen-hundred-year-old forest, when it has grown up and surrounded me on all sides. I do not need the proofs of its existence; it exists. So let us leave behind everything that was necessary at one time for the growth of the forest, for the formation of Christ's teaching.

Many things were necessary, but, after all, it is not a matter of investigating how the teaching was formed; the issue, rather, lies in the meaning of the teaching. The investigation of how the teaching was formed is a matter for history, but an understanding of the meaning of the teaching does not require an examination of the methods used to confirm the truth of the teaching. These two aspects are sharply distinguished in all the Gospels; as I have said, all four Gos-

pels are like a wonderful painting, which, for temporary
ends, has been covered with a layer of dark paint. This layer
extends over both sides of the painting. There is a layer over
one bare wall, before the birth of Christ (all the legends
about John the Baptist, about his conception and birth); then
there is a layer over the painting (the miracles, prophecies,
and predictions) and a layer over the other bare wall (the
legends of the resurrection, the Acts of the Apostles, and so
on). Knowing the thickness of the layer and its composition,
one must scrape it off the bare wall, particularly where it
clearly concerns the legend of the resurrection, and carefully
strip it from the whole painting. Only then shall we understand it in all its significance, and this is precisely what I have
attempted to do.

My reasoning is as follows: The Gospel consists of two
distinct parts, according to their aims. One is an account of
the teaching of Christ; the other is the proof of the importance and divinity of the teaching. The proofs of the importance and divinity of Christ's teaching are based on an
awareness of the truth of Christ's teaching (about which all
the churches are in exact agreement) and on external, historical proofs of the significance, importance, and divinity of the
teaching; collected into the Gospels during the initial times of
the teaching and powerful in their essence, these proofs are
convincing only to eyewitnesses. But in our times, they
achieve the opposite result and alienate people from an understanding and faith in the teaching of the Church—people
who are not the enemies of Christ but who are sincerely
devoted to the teaching. Nor can the churches help but agree
that the purpose of these proofs of the importance is the
persuasion of the truth of the teaching and that if there
should arise another, not internal but an external, historical
proof of the importance of the teaching—complete, irrefutable, and clear—then we must abandon those proofs that

arouse disbelief and serve as an obstacle to the spread of the teaching and must hold to the irrefutable and clear external proof of the importance. Such proof, which did not exist in the initial times, is the spread of the teaching itself, which penetrates all human knowledge, serves as the foundation of human life, and is constantly spreading. Thus, in order to understand the teaching, one not only can but inevitably must remove from the teaching all those proofs of its truth, which are replaced by other, indubitable proofs, which offer nothing to the comprehension of the teaching, and which serve as the chief obstacle to the acceptance of the teaching. Even if these proofs were not harmful, they are obviously no longer necessary, since they have a completely different purpose and can add nothing to the teaching.

THE END

About the Translator

AVID PATTERSON is Associate Professor of Russian, Oklahoma State University. He received his B.A., M.A., and Ph.D. from the University of Oregon. He is author of *The Shriek of Silence: A Phenomenology of the Holocaust Novel* (1992), *In Dialogue and Dilemma with Elie Wiesel* (1991), *The Affirming Flame: Religion, Language, Literature* (1988), *Literature and Spirit: Essays on Bakhtin and His Contemporaries* (1988), *Faith and Philosophy* (1982), and the translator of *Winter Notes on Summer Impressions* by F. M. Dostoevsky (1988), *The Forged Coupon* by Leo Tolstoy (1984), *Diary of a Superfluous Man* by Ivan Turgenev (1984), and *Confession* by Leo Tolstoy (1983).